ROUTLEDGE LIBRARY EDITIONS:
EARLY YEARS

Volume 9

NUMBER IN THE NURSERY AND INFANT SCHOOL

NUMBER IN THE NURSERY AND INFANT SCHOOL

EVELYN E. KENWRICK

LONDON AND NEW YORK

First published in 1937 by Routledge & Kegan Paul Ltd

This edition first published in 2023
by Routledge
4 Park Square, Milton Park, Abingdon, Oxon OX14 4RN

and by Routledge
605 Third Avenue, New York, NY 10158

Routledge is an imprint of the Taylor & Francis Group, an informa business

© 1937 Evelyn E. Kenwrick

All rights reserved. No part of this book may be reprinted or reproduced or utilised in any form or by any electronic, mechanical, or other means, now known or hereafter invented, including photocopying and recording, or in any information storage or retrieval system, without permission in writing from the publishers.

Trademark notice: Product or corporate names may be trademarks or registered trademarks, and are used only for identification and explanation without intent to infringe.

British Library Cataloguing in Publication Data
A catalogue record for this book is available from the British Library

ISBN: 978-1-032-34369-3 (Set)
ISBN: 978-1-032-35667-9 (Volume 9) (hbk)
ISBN: 978-1-032-35674-7 (Volume 9) (pbk)
ISBN: 978-1-003-32795-0 (Volume 9) (ebk)

DOI: 10.4324/9781003327950

Publisher's Note
The publisher has gone to great lengths to ensure the quality of this reprint but points out that some imperfections in the original copies may be apparent.

Disclaimer
The publisher has made every effort to trace copyright holders and would welcome correspondence from those they have been unable to trace.

NUMBER IN THE NURSERY AND INFANT SCHOOL

By
EVELYN E. KENWRICK
Author of *The Child from Five to Ten*

With a Foreword by
P. B. BALLARD, M.A., D.Litt.
late Divisional Inspector under the
London County Council

LONDON
ROUTLEDGE & KEGAN PAUL LTD
BROADWAY HOUSE: 68–74 CARTER LANE, E.C.4

First published 1937
Reprinted 1949
Reprinted (with some alterations) 1957
Reprinted 1963

Printed in Great Britain by Butler & Tanner Ltd, Frome and London

In this centenary year of the founding of the Kindergarten
I dedicate this book
TO MY STUDENTS
And to the memory of Our Greatest Froebelian
ELSIE RIACH MURRAY
who first inspired me to work out a modern interpretation
of Froebel's Principles.

CONTENTS

CHAP.		PAGE
	PREFACE	ix
	NOTE	xi
I.	GENERAL PRINCIPLES	1
II.	NUMBER IN THE NURSERY SCHOOL, THREE–FIVE YEARS	13

I : Play and Constructive Interests. II : Rhythmic Interests. III : Number Work of a more Abstract Nature.

III. NUMBER ARISING FROM PROJECTS . 60

I : Shops. II : 'Buses. III : Festivals, e.g. Christmas. IV : Lunch or Party Equipment. V : The Zoo. VI : The Street. VII : The Post Office. VIII : Development of an Estate Leading to Bank. IX : Dramatic Properties.

IV. NUMBER AS A SUBJECT . . . 86

Simple Addition and Subtraction.

V. THE MEASURING UNIT 12 . . . 103

A : The Dozen as Measured by the 12 Articles. B : The Shilling as Measured by the 12 Pennies.

VI. THE MEASURING UNIT 12 (*continued*) . 117

C : The Foot Rule as Measured by 12 Inches. D : The Clock Measured by the 12 Hours. E : The Year Measured by the 12 Months.

VII. WEIGHTS AND MEASURES . . . 140

A : Linear Measure. B : Avoirdupois—The Pound and Ounce. C : Measure of Capacity—The Pint, Quart, Gill, Half-pint. Summary.

VIII. FRACTIONS 156

I : Concrete Situations. II : Concrete Material. III : Individual Occupations.

CONTENTS

CHAP.		PAGE
IX.	NOTATION	164
	I: Concrete Situations. II: Concrete Material. III: Writing Numbers. IV: Numbers beyond 9.	
X.	ADDITION AND SUBTRACTION OF LARGER NUMBERS	183
	I: Concrete Situations. II: Concrete Material. III: Individual Occupations.	
XI.	ADDITION AND SUBTRACTION OF MONEY	200
	I: Concrete Situations. II: Concrete Material. Subtraction of Money.—I: Concrete Situations. II: Concrete Material.	
XII.	MULTIPLICATION TABLES . . .	211
	I: Concrete Situations. II: Concrete Material. III: Individual Occupations.	
XIII.	MULTIPLICATION AND DIVISION . .	219
	I: Concrete Situations. II: Concrete Material. III: Individual Occupations. Division.—I: Division by Measuring.—II: Division by Sharing. Multiplication and Division of Money.	
XIV.	SOME PRACTICAL SUGGESTIONS . .	239
	I: Concrete Material. II: Individual Occupations. Class Organization. Written Work.	
	CONCLUSION	246
	INDEX	247

PREFACE

THE most obvious fact about the teaching of number in the Infant School is that it shifts and changes. It is not to-day what it was yesterday; it is not the same in school *A* as it is in school *B*. A variety of influences has been at work in the Infant Schools and has given rise to a variety of methods and creeds. All teachers agree that it is vitally important that the earliest steps should be right; but they do not agree as to which are the right steps. Some, influenced by the teachings of Froebel, believe that if the children deal with concrete material, and deal with it in the spirit of play, then all will be well; others, under the influence of Montessori, believe that early individual work with special didactic apparatus will put the child on the right road; others, again, follow Dewey and pin their faith in projects. And there can be no doubt that each of these methods is in itself good; each has something to contribute to a complete solution of the problem. At the same time each is, in itself, incomplete. Indeed, all of them together are incomplete. Unless these " enlightened " modes of approach are followed by a certain measure of old-fashioned drill and memorization the full benefit of the course cannot be secured.

It is the outstanding merit of Miss Kenwrick's book that it recognizes all this. She surveys the whole field and gives to each factor its right place and value.

She shows which should come first, and why. She indicates the sequence most likely to make the subject organic—to make it a real part of the child's mental life. And in so doing she earns the gratitude of all those who try to guide the first faltering steps of the young mathematician.

Miss Kenwrick has written this book, not as an inexperienced theorist, but as one who has for many years been closely associated with Infant School work. She has trained teachers for that work and has carefully observed the results of different methods of teaching. In other words, the methods she prescribes are demonstrably practical. They " deliver the goods ". Nor are they merely practical—merely rule of thumb. For the principles upon which they are based are clearly and logically expounded.

I heartily commend this book to all teachers of the very young. It is lucid, it is abundantly helpful; it is in full accord with modern psychological theory.

P. B. BALLARD.

NOTE

PERHAPS the title of this book calls for comment. It is not suggested that the processes of the first four rules should be perfected in the Infant School. Complete ease in multiplication and division, involving as it does, the mechanization of the tables, will not be attained usually until the age of 8 or 9. As Professor Burt points out in the Psychological Appendix to the Primary Report, there is a natural aptitude for, and delight in, such routine-memory drills at this age. It is the work of the Junior School to complete the structure, building on the foundations, well and truly laid in the Infant School, of experience and discovery. Mental capacity differs widely between child and child; and " The range of work that is practicable will naturally vary with the capabilities of individual children. No uniform standard should be expected, but each child should be allowed to go as far as he is capable of going at his own rate of progress " (*Infant and Nursery School Report*, p. 136).

Much of the subject-matter of this book appeared in *Child Education* in 1935, and the articles are reprinted in this form by the courtesy of the Editor. The articles are reproduced at the request of many readers.

My grateful thanks are due to my sister Miriam and to Miss Mary Hickling for all the help they have so generously given.

E. E. K.

NUMBER IN THE NURSERY AND INFANT SCHOOL

CHAPTER I

GENERAL PRINCIPLES

In the everyday life of a little child before it goes to school there are many practical applications of number. Counting, comparing, measuring are natural interests arising out of the activities of the daily round. One of his earliest pleasures has been to hear the nursery rhymes and jingles which recite the numbers in sequence, and soon he counts the people at table, the cups, mats, and plates. In his endless journeys up and down the stairs, he chants the numbers with unwearied zest. Standing back-to-back with other children, lifting them off their feet, give the first attempts at comparison in height and weight. These activities act as stimuli and foster the growth of the child's earliest mathematical concepts. The fact that they are common to all normal children is sound evidence that Number is an absorbing interest of early childhood, and that the unmathematical child is rarely found in these pre-school years.

So the little child arrives at school with a primitive knowledge of number, using such terms as a lot, a few, little, bigger, older, heavier. This is the raw material from which the foundations of his mathematical education may and should be fashioned and developed. It is in the child's possession, it has been obtained in a happy natural way, and yet some vital link between this and the next stage is lost. For few teachers will deny that the teaching of arithmetic is one of the bugbears of the curriculum. The early interest flags and fades, till the avenues of progress are blocked in the middle forms with the hosts of the unmathematical, while the mathematical child seems a rare and heaven-born prodigy. Why this waste? Experiments many and varied have been made, and methods have been changed in the hope that these failures may be retrieved, but number teaching still remains a difficulty.

Let us examine some of the methods used in Infant Schools and Kindergartens in a serious endeavour to discover where the leakage is, and how this living interest has been dissipated before the Junior and Middle Schools are reached. At the same time we must look for principles, for methods are valueless unless they are based upon sound principles, intelligently grasped, and logically carried through.

The first type of teaching we will consider is seen in those schools where children use " sum " books. Columns of figures are entered into these books, and a similar copy is put upon the blackboard. Children and teacher work together, adding up the columns and writing " answers " to the sums. Gradually proficiency is achieved in one-column sums, and then they

GENERAL PRINCIPLES

are introduced to a dark mystery called " carryings ". A right-hand column is found to add up to 14, the instructions are to " put down 4 and carry 1 ". Now the left-hand column, totalling 11, becomes 12 by the addition of the carrying figure which has been " left out in the cold ". Subtraction, likewise, by the use of some such formula as " borrow 1, call it 10, 10 and 4 make 14, take 8 from 14 and it leaves 6 ", becomes the precarious possession of the bewildered child. The further processes by these rule-of-thumb methods are acquired, and the children gain a certain power of juggling with numbers and arriving at correct results.

There is no doubt that some pleasure is gained from this mechanical training in the mastery of rules, for parents and teachers testify that children often work pages of such sums in their own time for the sheer joy of the work. "Curiouser and curiouser " is probably their own inmost comment as they go from stage to stage of this extraordinary puzzledom, but the failure of this method is soon discovered by that ghostly detective —problem work—for no appeal has been made in the earlier work to the powers of reasoning, and problems have a sinister habit of dodging about so that one never knows which " rule " to apply !

Let us now turn to a consideration of the teaching given in those schools where concrete material in the shape of sticks, beans, counters, etc., has been introduced. With such apparatus the children are supposed to be able to work problems and sums. Number principles are demonstrated and explained to the class as a whole by means of this concrete material, and it is claimed that, as each child handles and arranges its own materials, the principles enunciated become clear as daylight—or any other luminous medium.

Then there are teachers who attribute failure in the teaching of number to the mass methods used. Individual methods, they urge, are the only way to a successful handling of the problem, and this is the way they go to work. Sum cards, bearing such mystic signs as $3 + 2 =$, $4 + 3 =$, are chosen by the children. They are *shown* how to work these sums with the aid of concrete material, and are then left to work by themselves. It is maintained that these children, being left free to work at their own pace and for any length of time, will somehow absorb and assimilate the principles of mathematics, like air and sunlight. But the mode of presentation of the material is the same, the only real difference between schools with class-teaching methods and those using individual methods is in the class organization. Whatever the method, a breakdown is inevitable sooner or later, for the children are dealing with a *subject* known as arithmetic. Concrete material may be brought in to aid them in grappling with the abstract principles involved, but the fact remains that they are concerned with a *subject*.

How does all this compare with the manner of life and education of the pre-school child? We have seen that he *had* mathematical concepts when he first came to school, and an examination of the way in which he gained them will afford us a series of clues to the natural workings of the child mind. From these we can derive basic principles for the subsequent teaching of number.

Primitive though these early ideas of number may be, they are the child's, for they have a meaning for him. The little child did not count, measure, weigh in order to learn a *subject* called number. *Interest* was the driving force of all his activities giving him the desire for *experiences*, and the acquisition of number was a by-product in the process. Sensory, or concrete, materials played their part by means of which he was provided with experiences, but they were not an end in themselves. Consequently the mathematical education had been incidental and informal. Now the school, in setting out with the " rotten tradition "[1] of teaching a subject called arithmetic, ignores the solid foundation principles from which the good work of pre-school years proceeded. The teacher concerns herself with the principles underlying the study of the subject, and relegates to the background the principles of the study of the child mind.

The child has to fit into the subject which " abstracts and analyses one set of facts and from one particular point of view. . . . Facts are torn away from their original place in experience and rearranged with reference to some general principle. Classification is not a matter of child experience ; things do not come to the individual pigeon-holed. . . . The studies as

[1] Caldwell Cook, *The Play Way*, p. 11.

classified are the product, in a word, of the science of the ages, not of the experience of the child ".[1]

Progressive teachers, who bear in mind these facts, have been trying yet other methods in the last few years. There are two main parties in the camp—those who still teach arithmetic as a subject yet keep an open mind for better ways of teaching, and on the other hand those who look solely to the children's interests and experiences to guide them in the right direction.

Recently another guiding-star has appeared above the educational horizon—the project method. Those fervent spirits, who have sighed for fresh light on the old and pressing problems, have hailed it as the ideal *modus operandi* for teacher and child. Especially for number teaching by the project method is a rich and vigorous harvest forecast, and as that is our chief concern here it will be well to state what is implied in this method. Briefly it is based upon a living principle, that of putting the child and his interests at the heart of the curriculum and allowing the work of education to revolve round this living centre. The centre of gravity in the sphere of education is thus shifted from the mass of subject-matter to the vital interests of the child. These are now seen to be the serious business of education, for, by means of these interests and the purposive activities connected with them, the child enters upon its inheritance of experience and knowledge. Seeing that in the project method

[1] Dewey, *The School and the Child*, pp. 20, 21.

GENERAL PRINCIPLES 7

subjects are not handled as subjects, its ardent supporters say that arithmetic as a subject must pass. Expensive patented apparatus is not called for, hence the sweeping assertion that " Individual apparatus and material are no longer necessary, experience is all that the children require ".

An example of a project may help us to see how such extremist views underestimate the needs of the children and bring the project method into disrepute, unless care is taken to build on experiences, and lead to knowledge and skills necessary for life. For example, in the constructive work for a zoo made by a class of six-year-old children, the children's primitive experiments in measuring led to the need for units of measure, thus :—

Bars for cages—cutting lengths of cane for boxes.
Doors of cages—made in relation to the height of animals.
Cover for catalogue—in this they had their first introduction to a unit of measure. A 9 in. length of cardboard was given to each child, to find the length required for the cover.
Tickets—for these, two strips of cardboard were used as units, one for length and another for width.
Hats for Keepers—paper was at first wound round the heads until a child remarked, " We want a tape-measure."

Thus the children were pursuing a living interest and at the same time gaining mathematical experiences. But the experiences alone could not *teach* the children how to measure, the relation of one measure to another, or their tables of measurement ; so the teacher, taking the foot rule as her unit evolved from these experiences a systematic course of lessons on measurement.

The problem, then, is to bridge the gulf between the

child's experience and interests, and the school's formulated study of subject-matter.

Professor Dewey says we must get rid of the prejudicial notion that there is " some gap in kind (as distinct from degree) between the child's experience and the various forms of subject-matter that make up the course of study. From the side of the child, it is a question of seeing how his experience already contains within itself elements—facts and truths—of just the same sort as those entering into the formulated study ". When we give up the bad old conception of subject-matter as ready-made, fixed, outside the child's experience, we shall regard it as " fluent, embryonic, vital ", then we shall realize that " the child and the curriculum are simply two limits which define a single process. Just as two points define a straight line, so the present standpoint of the child and the facts and truths of studies define instruction ".[1]

This is the problem before the educator to harmonize the child's experiences with subject-matter ; and—to quote Dewey again—if psychological considerations are put on one side they cannot be crowded out, " Put out of the door they come back through the window."[2] Motive must be sought and called in to aid by linking up the mind to its material, for when there is a lack of such incentive to action, and material is only supplied in lesson form, we shall see the spontaneous and living work of early childhood replaced by mechanical and lifeless forms.

[1] Dewey, *School and Child*, pp. 25, 26.   [2] Ibid., p. 42.

GENERAL PRINCIPLES 9

A project, by providing a motive or driving force, establishes the connection between the mind and its material, just as in the early years experience and interest sent the child in quest of further experience. But a project only undertakes to *motivate* the child's living interests, it cannot *teach* number or any other subject. Further steps have to be taken so that these experiences may be harnessed and driven into subjects.

In Number teaching the steps are, first, interest, then experience ; and this whatever the age of the children, or the processes they are concerned in learning. Unless concrete experiences supply the motive and show the need for the abstract work of the subject, the teaching will remain meaningless and abstract. And to bridge successfully the gap between home life and school, fresh and ever-widening experiences must be provided for the children. Activity, for its own sake, was the method of gaining experience in the child's home life, purposeful activity should supply it with further experiences in school.

Projects, or other play adventures, will provide concrete situations for purposeful activity in arithmetic ; reproducing life situations, the satisfying of play needs as seen in keeping shops, riding in 'bus and tramcar, playing at scoring games, etc. By all such means is Number motivated and the child's interest in it utilized.

Scholastic methods then can be placed in their true context by grasping " the necessity of more fundamental and persistent modes of tuition ".[1] Rightly directed concrete experiences will become a driving force and will lead to the study of the *subject* known as arithmetic, which will arise naturally to take its rightful place in the curriculum of the Infant School.

Experiences which have motivated number teaching must be supplemented by further experiences for the purpose of enlarging and enlightening the original experiences. Definite and systematic teaching with concrete material should *follow* concrete experience and bring with it opportunities for discovery and knowledge. By these means a balance between the informal and formal, the incidental and intentional in education is maintained.

Concrete experiences rightly handled will arouse a consciousness of ignorance, and studies with concrete material will now serve as a stepping-stone to the purely abstract. The children, with the aid of counters, bricks, bundles of sticks, or any other concrete apparatus, can be led to a discovery of the principles underlying the process to be studied, to meet the need they have come to feel.

This then is the order :—

1. *Concrete experiences* through projects or play experiences. These give the motive, the reason for, and the meaning to number work.

2. *Concrete material* when definite number teaching is given to enable the children to discover principles for themselves.

In this way intelligence and reasoning power are appealed to primarily, and mechanical memory is

[1] Dewey, *Democracy and Education*, p. 5.

GENERAL PRINCIPLES 11

relegated to the background. But memory must not be left there, neglected and forgotten, for it plays an important part in the mastery of processes by which they become the child's possession in reality. This leads on to yet another aspect of number teaching, that of memory work.

Desiring to release children from the drudgery which memory work was supposed to entail, there was a tendency for a time to dispense with this very important part of the work. It is possible to overstress the difficulties and dangers of committing to memory, but sound number teaching must include abstract drill work. By a neglect of this we err seriously, for a child needs prolonged experience with the facts of number to impress them on the mind, to have them pigeon-holed in the mind, ready to be recalled automatically as required for the consideration of further processes. The laws of habit, of attention, of memory must all have their share in stabilizing the good work begun through experience and discovery, and here is the justification for individual occupations in number work.

It will be noted that the term " Individual Occupations " is used instead of the usual " Individual apparatus ". This distinction between apparatus and occupations is purposely made—the former representing material used to stimulate reasoning power, while the latter term covers drill work and its aim is to aid memory. Individual occupations are usually for practice work, a mechanical sharpening of tools for further experiments.

Individual occupations do not teach arithmetic and if employed for this purpose they are mischievous and formal. As practice work they are valuable, and their appeal to the children lies in their attractiveness and variety, by means of which the drudgery of memory work is lightened. Confidence and joy are the outcome of these individual occupations, for they can be arranged and adapted to suit all types of mind with their varying rates of speed and output.

To sum up : The number interest of early childhood is developed in school—

(*a*) by means of concrete experiences, leading to

(*b*) a study of principles through concrete material or apparatus,

(*c*) and finally fixed in memory by practice work with individual occupations.

By proceeding, in this way, from life situations to the study of principles supplemented by practice work, thus are the stages in the teaching of Number balanced.

CHAPTER II

NUMBER IN THE NURSERY SCHOOL, THREE–FIVE YEARS

"The whole purpose of life, for me, being no philosopher, is simply living.

"It must have occurred to everyone that since a child's life under his own direction is conducted all in play, whatever else we want to interest him in should be carried out in that medium, or at the very least connected with play as closely as possible."[1]

"Play and living," the inner urge and purpose of life for the three–five-year old—as shown in his love of constant movement and incessant activity—were ruled out when compulsory education came in. Mental activity, it was maintained, could only be achieved by the inhibition of bodily and muscular movements. Those teachers who loved children and dimly realized the pathetic results of this repression of the play instincts, gradually introduced into the curriculum certain activities as little rewards for the accomplishment of the schoolday's drudgery. These experiments were not made to awaken mental activity or to work in harmony with it, they were unrelated luxuries for *real work done*. To-day, the voluntary attention and muscular inhibitions demanded of children in the past

[1] Caldwell Cook, *Play Way*, p. 14.

are known to harm and cramp every side of their nature.

The Nursery School Report, recognizing that activity is a *need* of the little child, and that the Nursery and Infant Schools exist " to cater for the needs of infancy ", demands that every possible provision for activity be made. The children of the Nursery School must have freedom to respond to the dictates of their own nature, to move about at will, choosing their own occupations and following their own interests by means of play. Their teacher has the most difficult post in the school, and needs the highest skill to justify her presence as guide and providence in this department, willing to sit still or to stand away from the children ; a teacher who does not teach, yet holds herself in readiness for any emergency, so important and yet so superfluous ! Surely at no other stage in its school life does the child demand so much from, and again so absolutely disregard, his self-forgetting, self-effacing helper. It is true that the teacher in the Nursery School has not to prepare systematic schemes of work or to cover so much ground in a year, but from a constant watching of the children's reactions she has to see that they are developing and gaining mentally, physically, socially, and spiritually.

In our first chapter we considered several examples of babyhood's interest in number. We noted the love of counting and rhythmical experiences, and discovered that through these the fundamental number concepts are gained.

NUMBER IN THE NURSERY SCHOOL 15

The teachers in the Nursery School should know their children's interests and provide a variety and abundance of material, which can be employed in purposeful ways, e.g. estimating, selecting, shaping, and adapting to ends. The children's interest in number must be utilized in every possible way, in play, games, rhythm, jingle, and song with a teacher who knows how to play, while the children should find opportunities for satisfying their number interests and gaining concrete experiences from which more definite number teaching can be developed later. Number must not be thought of apart from the children; in these early years the training will be of the informal incidental kind, and arising as they do from the children's interests the experiences will of necessity be of a haphazard order.

The following suggestions, taken from my students' notebooks, have been worked out in the Nursery Classes of the Elementary School, and are classified for the sake of convenience under the following headings :—

        I. Play and Constructive Interests.
       II. Rhythmic Interests.
      III. Abstract Number Interests.

Number arises out of these interests, and at this point we do not attempt to differentiate between the three stages of Number teaching (noted in our first chapter), for the three merge into one, and the teacher's work is to watch for opportunities whereby the ideas of number may be elucidated and better defined.

I. Play and Constructive Interests

1. *Play-houses*

" It is life that educates," might well be inscribed over the play-houses which are now a common feature of our Nursery Schools.

How great is the contrast between the education of yesterday and to-day may be realized if one watches the happy little ones busily occupied with various domestic occupations in school. Yes ! in school, for it can in truth now be affirmed that the schools, whose " first intention it was to teach children how to read, have been compelled to broaden their aims until it might now be said that they have to teach children how to live ".[1] For the aim and purpose of education are now felt to be gained and served by strengthening and enlarging the children's " instinctive hold on the conditions of life by enriching, illuminating, and giving point to their growing experience "[2]; and knowledge is acquired, and facts stored only through those incidental experiences which are taken in the stride of purposeful play activities.

We aim now at showing how, under wise guidance, the incidental experiences of a play-house may engender and foster the Number interest and, to illustrate our points, we will describe such a play-house recently placed in a Nursery Class. The house in question was improvised from clothes-horses covered with curtains discarded from the teacher's home. Chairs and tables were carried into this house, and old boxes

[1] *The Primary Report*, p. 93. [2] Ibid., p. 93.

NUMBER IN THE NURSERY SCHOOL 17

were quickly converted into a dresser and a cupboard. Here, the little ones lived a busy, " human " life with their dolls and toys, and, as they played, their teacher, on tip-toe with intelligent anticipation, supplemented the domestic equipment further with such materials and utensils as she saw were needed to stimulate the interest in number and to keep it up to the maximum.

Meals were served at all hours, and though the hospitality was free and easy, it could hardly be considered of the " Quick Lunch " variety. In the silver basket were to be found spoons, forks, and knives ; six of each, cut in cardboard to the regulation sizes—table, dessert, and tea ; on the dresser, the same number of plates, also in three sizes—meat, pudding, and tea—were to be found. The cupboard contained six tea, and six breakfast cups which could be matched to saucers of corresponding sizes, and in this cupboard were also to be found jugs of three sizes. Table-laying did not become a fine art until there had been numerous attempts and haphazard journeys, which resulted in cupboards, dresser, and silver basket being cleared. Then knowledge superseded random experiment, and the children considered guests in relation to their needs, and counts were made of the various utensils required, the grand total also being worked out for the sheer joy of reckoning. Sometimes food, made from dough or plasticine, was served ; but on other occasions, conkers and acorns were offered as dainties, and the spontaneous exclamations of " What a lot ", as plates were piled up, attracted the teacher and her desire to find out " How many ? " led to children and teacher helping each other to count. As the food was served, it was evident that the number aspect made an appeal, for the children would often pause to count how many of the big and how many of the little nuts were on the plates, and how many were left on dishes.

The same interest in number was evident as " tea " (water) was poured into the cups, but it required many repetitions of the activity to convince the children that the jugs of different sizes filled cups of different numbers and sizes.

> *Number Involved.*
> *Counting*—Utensils, guests, nuts, acorns, conkers.
> *Size*—Utensils, nuts, acorns, etc.
> *Capacity*—Amount of liquids for different vessels.

Constructive Work : Rebuilding the House.

The play-house was looking dingy ! This æsthetic consideration very likely would never have arisen had not the teacher, on the return journey from playground to the school one day, paused by the school wall and, passing her hand and fingers over the brickwork and along the lines of mortar, remarked, " Our house has not bricks like these, I wish it had." This acted as the suggestion for reconstructing the house, but before this could be attempted, bricks had to be made. From the school stock of building blocks, bricks of uniform size were found by the children while the teacher looked on, and wondered at the vague notions of volume displayed by the children, who found themselves up

NUMBER IN THE NURSERY SCHOOL 19

against a problem in deciding which were alike in length, breadth, and width.

Bricks, of the same dimensions, having at length been separated into one pile, the children each took a brick, and, using it as a template, drew, coloured, and cut out bricks for the house. As they worked, so they counted. While this occupation was in progress, the teacher stripped the house in readiness for reconditioning (for the children realized the impossibility of using the curtain material for a background for the bricks); then, helped by small groups of children—chosen because of their better developed control of hand and muscle—the house was measured by placing pads of newspaper against the framework, to which the pads were then nailed.

Before proceeding with the work of bricklaying, further excursions to the playground were made, and new thrills were experienced as the children traced with their hands the arrangement of the bricks, and noted the position of fingers when tracing out the horizontal and vertical lines of the mortar. In this way, the building of the house progressed, and it was apparent that interest in number was as great as ever, for tools were often laid aside while counts of bricks already in place were made, and the area of surfaces covered compared with the extent of the parts still to be completed.

Number Involved.
  Volume—Sorting bricks from brick box.
  Counting—Piles of bricks cut, and bricks pasted.
  Lines—Horizontal and vertical.

Further Play in the Play-house

It is almost a truism to say that in an atmosphere which fosters full and complete living, monotony has no place, and this is proved up to the hilt in the Nursery Classes with their crowded hours of joyous living. In the great outside world, different uses are suggested by different materials and equipment and, in the microcosm of the Infant School, apparatus spontaneously generates ideas in the minds of teachers and children, for its use in a variety of ways. Thus it was with the play-house. Though it was built and equipped for individual and free play, the teacher saw further, and seized other opportunities presented in the story periods for quickening the children's number interests and stirring dramatic impulses. At this age, the child's knowledge of, and interest in, the world are bounded by and centred in the activities and lives of those immediately about him. Realizing this, the teacher wove the adventures of the house's occupants into an exciting story, which introduced the various callers supplying the household wants day by day, and thus filled the stage with actors.

A family of mother, father, and two children were chosen to take possession of the house. In various parts of the room, a milkman, postman, and travelling greengrocer staked their claims, where they set out their proper equipment for giving service and satisfaction to their customers. The rest of the class sat on chairs or the floor, facing the house and listened spellbound to the story with its simple plot, such an

NUMBER IN THE NURSERY SCHOOL 21

easy " take-off " for the imaginative flights in which they followed all the well-known adventures of the familiar characters in this serial. While developing her story, the teacher identified herself with the different people, and in mime led the children to personify them too. Dramatic interest thus stimulated, the children were able to take an active part either as principals or understudies, in the lively experiences of these important folk.

For this story-acting-number period, the teacher brought to the class the following apparatus :—

A push-bell to be used in conjunction with a clock face.
A postman's bag containing 12 or more letters.
A toy milk-cart on which were milk bottles of three sizes (quart, pint, ½-pint) filled with " milk ", prepared by stirring a little whitening into water.
A parcel postman's hand-cart with dummy parcels of different sizes and weights—*heavy* parcels, large and small; *light* parcels, large and small; *medium-sized* parcels, heavy and light.
A greengrocer's barrow with scales and vegetables, etc., sold by weight or counts.

The story was introduced by the announcement, in a hushed voice, that it was night time when everyone was fast asleep in bed, " Mother, father, and the children in the house, the postman in his house, the milkman and greengrocer in their houses (pointing to each in turn), and all of us in our houses (closing her eyes and resting her cheek on her clasped hands)." In this position, all rested for a few seconds, then the story continued as follows :—

" 1, 2, 3, 4, 5, 6, 7 (striking 7 times on the push bell). It is 7 o'clock (pointing to the hands of the clock as they are put in position), time to get up. We wash our necks and ears, our hands and faces, and brush our hair (miming all these actions). Here comes the milkman. Look! He has brought one *large* bottle, one *small* bottle, and one *middle-sized* bottle of milk. Mother will answer the door when the milkman knocks, and tell the milkman which bottle she wants. Oh, see! She has taken the *large* bottle, *one quart* of milk. She wants it for breakfast, and perhaps she will have some left over to make a milk pudding."

Then follows the laying of the breakfast table, and all are sitting down to the meal when the clock strikes 1, 2, 3, 4, 5, 6, 7, 8, teacher and children counting and then noticing the clock face on which the hands now point to 8 o'clock. As the meal proceeds, either in play or mime form, the teacher calls the children's attention to the arrival of the postman. "Can you hear him coming up the street? 1, 2, 3, 4, etc., steps. Listen to him knocking at the door. How many letters is he going to drop through the letter-box? 1, 2, 3, 4, 5, 6, etc."

The story continues with the striking and counting of 9 o'clock, when the greengrocer's cart arrives on the scene, and so many bananas are bought, and potatoes weighed on the scales. Washing-up, dusting, bed-making, and other household occupations follow, and 10 o'clock is the time when the parcel postman strolls up the road with his parcels of varying sizes and weights, all of which are noted and handled by different children.

NUMBER IN THE NURSERY SCHOOL 23

This is but one suggestion for such a story planned to satisfy the children's triple interests of number, language, and acting. Others will suggest themselves to the teacher and be developed according to the needs of her class.

Number Involved.
    Counting—Strikes of the clock, number of letters delivered by the postman, greengrocer's counts.
    Quantity—In wet measure.
    Size and shape—Parcels and bottles.
    Weight—Balance in goods on scales, weight of parcels.

Constructive Work : Decorations and Furnishings.

The bricklaying occupations, already described, gave rise to the desire to paper the inside of the walls. So the teacher cut strips of wallpaper to the length of the framework, and on these the children made coloured patterns and then nailed them to the walls, counting as they went the number of pieces required for the width of the house. Great surprise was expressed when they found that so few strips were needed for so large an area !

Windows were cut out of the coverings by the teacher, though the areas required for the frames were estimated by the children, guided by the teacher's wise use of the terms " How long ? ", " How wide ? "

Now curtains—and from a pile of pretty tissue papers, the children chose what would " look nice " with their walls and then proceeded to find the required lengths by comparing them with the window-frames. A fresh problem in dealing with width had to be faced in hanging the curtains, and this was solved by

24 NUMBER IN THE NURSERY SCHOOL

the children with measures devised from string. This was also used for attaching the curtains, and here the teacher had to give some guidance, and show the children how to fold and paste a paper hem over the string.

It was now seen that something must be found for a window-sill and, after rummaging amongst the waste material, a piece of cardboard was pronounced to be

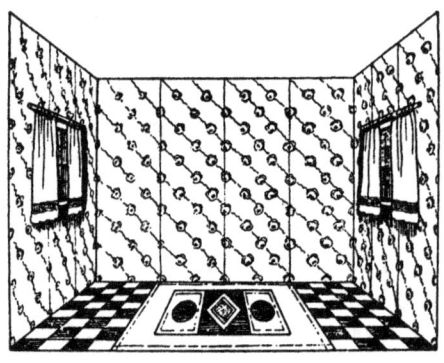

" about as long as " the window-frame. Here again many decisions of " not wide enough ", or " too wide " were made and reversed, before the right piece was satisfactorily chosen. The bending of the cardboard by a half-cut had to be done by the teacher, but the children nailed it to the framework.

Mats for the floor were made by pasting paper shapes on to a newspaper foundation, and this gave further experiences in area and fitting means to an end.

Number Involved.
Measurement—Length and width of wall papers, curtains, and window-sill.
Area—Wall and floor coverings.

2. *Doll Play*

There was no room for a play corner even, in another room crowded with more than fifty four-year-olds. The dual desks mounted on the " steps " of the old-fashioned classroom floor could only be left in formal rows, but the student in charge refused to be daunted. For three weeks the class played blissfully at " Mothers and fathers " with their gay young families of newspaper dolls, arrayed in crinkled paper dresses of every hue, imitating the social activities of their own surroundings.

(a) *Cooking*—*Ingredients*—beans, sand, clay, dough, and water.
Utensils—spoons, cups, jugs, patty pans, and scales.

With these they estimated weight, capacity, and balance, this last gave endless pleasure as the different goods were balanced one against the other in the two pans of scales.

(b) " *Let's pretend* " *tea parties*, led to counting and arranging as they planned food, table equipment, and seats for the expected number of guests.

(c) *Floral decorations* for the house called for arrangement and comparison. In choosing vases and the flowers suitable to different heights, they discovered that little flowers looked best in small vases, and so on. It was not comfortable for the flowers to be crowded so they experimented and found how many could fit into a vase satisfactorily. Another problem was suggested and solved—and much water spilled—when the jugs were used to fill the vases. For by measuring it was seen that one jugful filled the little vases, two the larger ones, and so on.

(d) Washing Day.

For this play tubs, soap-flakes, teaspoons, basins, two large jugs of warm water, several smaller jugs, a clothes-line and pegs were required. The children used the jugs to measure the water needed to fill the tub; with spoons they mixed a soap lather in a basin. Clothes were washed and hung out to dry with clothes-pegs on a line.

Number Involved.

Counting the clothes, pairs of socks, etc. Amount of water needed for filling the tub—so many jugsful. So many spoonsful of soap-flakes to make a lather for such a jug and for the tub. The clothes-line must be long enough to hang between two hooks. Numbers of pegs required for hanging out the clothes.

Constructive Work.

As they cared for the needs of the dolls, there were numerous constructive and number activities on the children's part which are tabulated below:—

Constructive Work.

(i) *Beds*, from boxes.

Number Involved.

Rough Measurement (by relating doll to box).

The children had to select a box to fit their doll from a pile of different sizes and shapes.

(ii) *Bedclothes*, from paper. Kitchen paper for sheet and blankets. Coloured tissue for bedspreads.

Rough Measurement.

The box bed was laid on the paper, drawn round, and then cut out.

(iii) *Mattresses*, from paper bags filled with shredded newspaper.

Rough Measurement.

From several bags of different sizes, the children chose one suitable for the mattress. The filling was judged with regard to comfort. "That mattress will not be comfortable, it has not enough stuffing in it."

"This one is better, it has more stuffing," etc.

NUMBER IN THE NURSERY SCHOOL

Constructive Work.
(iv) *Chairs*, from boxes.

Number Involved.
Rough Measurement.
The doll must be able to sit comfortably in its chair, which was measured and made accordingly.

(v) *Tables*, from boxes.

Rough Measurement.
The relation to the chair, and the doll sitting in it was considered.

(vi) *Tea Services.*
(a) *Plates and Saucers*, from paper.

Shape.
A circular object, e.g. an inverted saucer, placed on the paper, drawn round, and cut out.

(b) *Cups and jugs*, from cream cartons and decorated with cut paper motifs.

Measuring.
Selection of cartons according to sizes regarded suitable for cups and jugs.
Handles cut from paper.
Placing motifs for design.

(vii) *Tablecloths*, made from sheets of kitchen paper.

Measurement.
These were made in relation to the table which was used as a template.
A development was seen when the children wished the cloth to come over the edge of the table.
Flaps were added by sticking strips of paper round the sides of cloth, and these were found to be acceptable to the children at this age.

(viii) *Food.*
(a) *Cakes*, from plasticine. Coloured plasticine made most effective cakes; one colour, e.g. chocolate, chosen for the cake and others as pink, green, white for decoration.

Solids and shapes—
  The round ⎫
      square ⎬ cake
      oblong ⎭

Constructive Work.	Number Involved.
(b) *Biscuits* from plasticine.	*Shapes* square, oval, round, oblong.
	Counting and arranging on plates.
(c) *Bread and butter*, from post-cards.	*Shapes*—A square template was given to each child, the pieces cut from this were cut diagonally giving two triangles.
(d) *Drinks*, from water.	*Rough measuring of* liquids. Small jugs filled with water from a big jug on teacher's table.
	Cups filled from the small jugs.

The Dolls Go to the Seaside

Even the hot July days cannot exhaust the interests ever germinating and growing in the fertile minds of the children. As thought and conversation flit from the gay pictures on the classroom walls, and the alluring railway posters to the coming holidays and the joys of the seaside, the teacher gladly accepts the inspiration given, and seaside plays take the stage in every sense. " The dolls ought to go to the seaside," is the teacher's subtle suggestion as she sees opportunities for much work of an educational nature, and the game is taken up with alacrity. At first, the children follow their usual course and carry through any idea that rises at random. When they seek guidance, the teacher is ready with a broadly outlined scheme in which all may find a place, and play their part, and, instead of haphazard unconcerted actions, the game develops as follows :—

The mothers of the dolls collect and pack their (boot-box) trunks ; and the boys, with the help of the teacher, improvise a train with chairs drawn up beside a platform chalked along the floor. The requisite number of tickets for the outward journey are provided to stock the ticket office, which is arranged by placing one table on top of another. By the time the passengers arrive at the station with luggage and money for the journey, the booking-clerk is in his place. Porters are lined up to label and take luggage to the guard's van, or to find places in the carriages for the travellers ; and at last the guard, who has been standing with flag in hand, blows his whistle as he hears the last stroke of 8, struck by the town clock (a push bell).

Constructive Work in Connection with the Play.

Various enjoyments await the holiday makers on their arrival, and the children may be broken up into groups for the following plays involving constructive work and number.

1. The sand-trays offer endless occupation for the dolls to dig, make pies, or sand-castles. The gigantic pails used by human children are quite unsuitable for dolls, and some enterprising townsman may open a shop, where spades and pails are manufactured and sold (at a side table). For this purpose, cream cartons of several sizes may be converted quickly into pails, the children choosing from several lengths of solder the right sizes for threading through the two holes, previously pierced in the cartons. The two parts of

the spade should have been cut in cardboard in several sizes previously by the teacher, and the children select from the bundle of shapes those which fit together to make spades of good proportions.

2. Sea corners may be arranged on tables for groups of three or four children and their dolls. A sheet of sand-coloured paper meeting in the middle of the table blue paper irregularly edged, makes a realistic shore setting. As the dolls paddle, they fill their pails with shells and stones of various shapes and sizes, and, returning to arrange them on the beach, they find

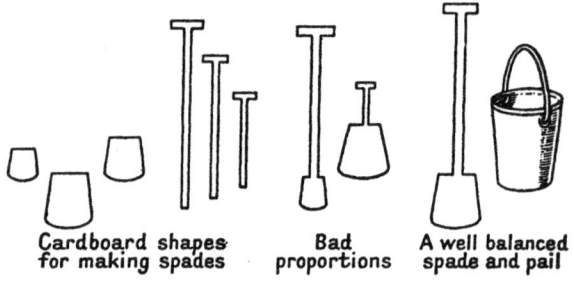

Cardboard shapes for making spades   Bad proportions   A well balanced spade and pail

that they have fewer or more stones or shells in their pails according to the size of the specimens they have picked up.

3. On the pier (a narrow area marked on the floor enclosed by chairs and looking out on to a sea of crêpe paper), dolls fish with bamboo rods on to the end of the string of which is tied a small magnet. Large, small, and medium-sized fish are cut from templates in cartridge paper, covered with silver paper, with a wire clip pushed through the mouth as an

NUMBER IN THE NURSERY SCHOOL 31

attraction to the magnet. Naturally, the doll fisher-folk are interested in the number of fish in their pails, and, without knowing it, the children get number experiences as they compare numbers and sizes in their hauls.

4. While the holiday-makers are thus enjoying their leisure, station officials are not forgetful of the return journey which will have to be made by the trippers, and more tickets may be made in preparation for this. The children's problem will be to see how many tickets they can get with a cardboard ticket used as a template on sheets of cartridge paper.

Number Involved in Play and Constructive Work.

Counting—Number of passengers travelling. Arranging seats for the train. The number of trunks in the guard's van. Tickets. Time—as struck by the clock for the departure of the train. Number of spades and pails. Number of fish caught.

Size—Sand castles and pies of various sizes. Pails and spades of different sizes related to each other. Fish of different sizes. Shells of different sizes.

Measurement—Length of handles of different sized pails. Two parts of spades selected in relation to each other. Fish of different lengths.

Money—Paying for tickets on railway. Paying for spades and pails—more money for larger than smaller ones.

Area—Station and platform, pier areas.

3. *Shops*

Small tables do very well for counter-tops, and if some shelves can be spared for a background the shop is the last word in realism. One class teacher nobly cleared the children's treasure-box shelf and handed it over to the student, thereby adding great zest to the play, and greater opportunities for number.

At this age, shopping consists solely in fetching goods from the shop and handing over the counter their cardboard money. The amount does not matter, it is enough now for the children to gain the idea of exchange.

"The play's the thing" for the children, and the teacher, while agreeing with the sentiment, helps to develop their experiences through it.

Shops and Goods Sold Therein.	*Number Involved.*
(i) *Sweetshop.*	
Sweets, made from—	*Counting.* The children count as they make and pack them in the boxes. Comparisons are made with numbers of sweets made by different children, and with numbers put into boxes of different sizes.
(a) Plasticine.	
(b) Newspaper rolled into small bolster shapes and covered with coloured crinkled papers (the teacher should prepare these covering squares of crinkled paper) and packed in—	
Boxes covered with wallpaper.	*Measurement.* The teacher prepares wallpaper shapes cut to fit the top and sides of the boxes.
	The children's problem is to select the right strip for the surface they have to cover.
(ii) *Grocery Store.*	
(a) Dummy packets and tins.	*Counting* numbers of tins.
	Arranging the tins according to size. Big ones at the back of the shelf or counter and small ones in front.

NUMBER IN THE NURSERY SCHOOL

Shops and Goods Sold Therein.

(b) Tins of dried goods for weighing.

Number Involved.

Weighing. Discovering the principle of balance, and terms " heavy ", " light," " the same."

(iii) *Greengrocer and Fruiterer.*
Fruits and vegetables, made from—
(a) Clay.
(b) Stiff paper or postcards. Hectographed outlines may be prepared by the teacher for the children to cut out in the double or made to stand by a strip of paper stuck on the back.

Counting and arranging.
Weighing—as in grocer's shop.

(iv) *Confectioner.*
For suggestions and number involved see section on doll play.

(v) *Dairy.*

(a) *Milk bottles* and *cartons*, to be filled with small jugs, from a bowl of water containing starch or ground chalk, to give a milky appearance.

Rough ideas of liquid measure.
Comparison of sizes and quantity required for vessels of different capacities.

(b) *Butter.* A slab of clay modelled with butter-pats or strips of lathwood.

Shapes. Children break off lumps of clay and model into forms with butter pats.
Weight. Children try to make pats of equal weight.

(vi) *Draper's Shop.*

(a) *Materials*, ribbons and laces of different lengths, colours and textures from the rag-bag.

Length. Comparison of lengths " a long, a short piece " — " A piece long enough for my doll's sash."
N.B.—The sense training with such materials.

(b) *Buttons*, real buttons or paper discs to be coloured.

Counting and arrangement on cards.

4. *Farms*

The small animals from Woolworth's supplemented by fields, hedges, and buildings, constructed by the teacher from waste material and cardboard, will provide all the thrills of a farm and much incidental number teaching while the true play progresses. A foreground, planned according to the accompanying diagram (or any other originated by the teacher), on to which shapes, hedges, and buildings are to be fitted, is given to the children. On each section of the plan, names may be printed corresponding to the names on the shapes and buildings. (This will also give word-matching experiences.) Buildings, shapes, and hedges have to be fitted into the correct places, and animals are grouped in the fields or led to the shelters—sometimes eight cows may be in the field, three are taken to be milked, when it is interesting to the little ones to find that five remain in the open.

Number involved—Counting and Grouping Animals.
  Fitting hedges round fields.
   Shapes to be found and fitted to correspond to those on the foreground—square, rectangular, oval, round.

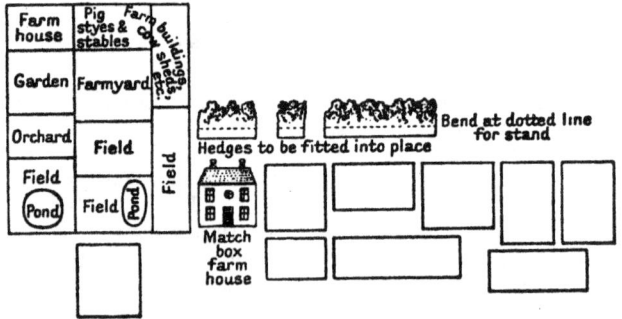

NUMBER IN THE NURSERY SCHOOL 35

Constructive Interests : Handwork for the Farm.

1. Making new fields from the teacher's shapes, which are used as templates for the children to draw round.

Number involved.
   Shapes—Square, oblong, round, oval.

2. Constructing new shelters for animals from waste material—boxes of different sizes.

Number involved.
   Size—Relating animals to boxes, e.g. the low pigstye, the stable big enough for three horses, etc.

5. *Flowers*

June's varied loveliness of colour and perfume should make this month a time of great enjoyment to teachers and children. Pinks and marigolds, roses and pansies, cornflowers, Canterbury bells, sweet-williams, larkspur, and thrift—and many others—throng the classrooms, brought to school in small and large bunches. As the teacher considers the due ordering of this mixed multitude, she sees the realization of her special aims of satisfying the children's love of beauty and increasing their understanding of nature's marvels, and may see even further opportunities for challenging and using the children's interest in number.

As flowers arrive on Monday morning, a tin or enamel bath, filled with water and placed on a table covered with American cloth, should be prepared for their reception. Jugs of water, jars, vases of different heights and sizes, and flat bowls (or tiny pie-dishes) filled with damp sand for violets and pansies, should also be on the table, ready for the arranging of the gifts.

In the large class, the difficulty of organization has to be faced and overcome ; and at first, collective work will be the most satisfactory solution. During this part of the lesson, the children may be called up in groups to enjoy the sight and scent of the flowers *en masse*, and after a few words, designed to bring home to the children the needs of flowers similar to their own, it is decided to separate the beautiful things and arrange them so that these needs may be met. Now, a group of children may be called out to count so many flowers—e.g. twelve—from the bath, eventually transferring them to the vases. The children's arrangements will result in some little flower-faces hardly showing above the edge of the vases ; and some of the long-legged tribes, fox-gloves, columbines, or cornflowers awkwardly and dangerously leaning over in small potted meat jars. As they try to rearrange and prop up, the children arrive at the idea of finding vases of suitable heights for the different specimens ; then the work becomes individual, as each child counts its flowers, fetches and fills the vase suited to its choice, and returning to its own place in the classroom arranges after its own plan.

Number involved.

Counting—so many (the number to be judged by the size of the vase).

Measurement—Comparison of lengths of stalks—with each other and with vases.

Capacity—Measuring so much water to fill the jugs.

NUMBER IN THE NURSERY SCHOOL 37

Constructive Work: Planning and Making the Garden.

When the arrangement of the flowers has been accomplished, tables wiped, any debris cleared away, and the children have had time to enjoy the contemplation of their handiwork, the teacher suggests that a garden might be planned in the classroom.

For garden beds, the teacher will have in readiness a number of rectangular tins or trays (in one school, during a period of settled, dry weather, a teacher borrowed the zinc trays of the umbrella stands for this purpose); templates of different rectangular shapes (square and oblongs); pieces of green and brown paper; paste and scissors.

The area of the garden is chalked on the classroom floor, and while some of the children find the right number of trays required to fit along the sides, the remainder occupy themselves drawing and cutting out with their templates shapes to fit on to the teacher's prepared backgrounds for grass and garden paths. The garden thus made ready for the flowers, the next step is for each child to place on the trays its own vase in the position it chooses. Admiration of the work then follows, then the teacher again throws out other suggestions as she notes that some of the smaller flowers are hidden by taller ones. Other arrangements are tried, and finally after many trials involving comparison of vases and flowers, it is decided to assemble all the tall vases at the back of the garden, the medium sizes in the middle, and the little flowers at the front.

Number involved.
> *Lengths and heights*—Measuring and comparing lengths of flowers and vases for the final arrangements of tall, short, and medium.
>
> *Area*—Fitting shapes on to the area allowed for grass and brown-paper paths.
>
> *Counting*—Finding the number of trays required for the sides of the garden.

6. *Acting*

Imitation and dramatization, so the psychologists tell us, play a large part in the activities connected with toys and plays at this age. The little ones love to dress up and assume the characters they see daily, or hear about in their stories, and if acting can be linked with the developed interest in housekeeping appliances, much may be done in the way of aiding and furthering still another interest, that of Number.

A Teddy bear, brought to school, may be introduced as the Baby Bear of the classics; and, as she tells her story, the teacher uses the toy, speaking with his tiny voice, copying his tiny footsteps, and at the same time comparing them with those of his parents. Realizing that here is a golden opportunity for dramatic language and number experiences, she may then suggest acting the story, and the children will set to work to furnish the home of the Three Bears. A table is placed in readiness, then chairs have to be arranged around it. The relation of the chairs to the size of the table will not concern the children, it will be found that they tend to concentrate on finding such as will answer

NUMBER IN THE NURSERY SCHOOL 39

to the descriptions in the story. "A very big chair ; a middle-sized chair ; a tiny little chair." From amongst utensils previously placed in different parts of the room by the teacher with prophetic vision, bowls and spoons for porridge will be selected. Before the final decisions are made, there will be much adjusting and fitting together, measuring and comparison by fitting into one another of salt cellars, pudding basins, and large round bowl or vegetable dishes ; salt-, tea-, dessert-, tablespoons, gravy and soup ladles, and all these operations make all kinds of demands upon mental and physical activity. Porridge basins may be filled from the damp sand of the sand tray, and the kitchen spoon, used as a measurer, will show that— " a lot of spoonfuls—1, 2, 3, 4, 5, 6,"—are necessary for filling Father Bear's big bowl ; " 1, 2, 3, 4—not so many," for Mother Bear's middle-sized bowl ; and " 1—only 1," for Baby Bear's tiny little bowl.

The breakfast table set and ready, attention is next directed to the bedroom, and Baby Bear's tiny bed may be prepared with two of the schoolroom chairs. Ignorant of its mathematical significance as a unit of measurement, but satisfied with the result as a tiny bed big enough for Baby Bear, a second, and a third, problem arise in consciousness, " Now, we want a middle-sized bed for Mother Bear ; and we shall want a *very* big bed for Father Bear." So chairs are arranged and rearranged until a satisfactory result is obtained by comparing with Baby Bear's bed. Six chairs, arranged in three lines of two, on which Mother Bear can lie comfortably ; nine chairs, arranged in three lines of three, may accommodate Father Bear. Bed coverings, improvised from sheets of newspaper, will lead to measuring of a primitive type. One sheet, placed lengthways, will be sufficient protection for Baby Bear ; two sheets for Mother Bear, and three sheets for Father Bear.

Stage and properties complete, anticipation rises high once more, for now the choice of cast has to be made. Principals cannot be nominated at random when, in answer to the question " Whom shall we have for Father Bear ? ", there is a chorus of " Have me," " I will ! ". " The story tells us," says the teacher, " that Father Bear was a *very* big Bear," and the children see the wisdom of transferring desires for self-display to the real problem of finding the tallest, by measuring all the boys back to back. In the same way, Mother Bear, is not necessarily the one who clamours for the part, but is chosen by solving the problem, " Who is the tallest girl ? "

So, when all is ready, the audience settles down in their places, and the teacher takes the part of narrator. In retelling her story, by her skilful choice of language, she draws out and guides the principals by her suggestions. Story and acting proceed simultaneously while the number aspect is well to the fore. " Once upon a time," and the description of the preparation for the morning walk is followed by, " Father Bear walks out of the house with 1—2—3—4—(very solemnly and slowly) big steps. Mother Bear follows, and takes

NUMBER IN THE NURSERY SCHOOL 41

1, 2, 3, 4, 5, 6, middle-sized steps. Then comes Baby Bear walking (recited quickly and in a squeaky voice) 1, 2, 3, 4, 5, 6, 7, 8 steps," etc.

Number involved.
Measuring—Chairs, spoons, bowls, beds, bed coverings. Heights of children. Amount of porridge in bowls.
Counting—Number of chairs for beds. Number of steps taken by the different Bears.

Constructive Work.

The eager pleas for "playing it again", are encouraged by the teacher, who knows the delight in repetition experienced by these little children, but after several repeat performances, she considers ways and means whereby this interest may be used to fulfil *her* purpose of furthering the children's intellectual and physical development.

The children's growing enthusiasm for constructive work suggests one possibility of such expansion. As she explains to the children that the borrowed utensils they are using will have to be returned to the kitchen, she asks them if they would not like to make their own permanent "properties". So, from modelling material, clay, or plasticine, bowls are made by rolling the material into balls, which are then hollowed out with fist or fingers. The finished work is assembled on a table, and the vessels grouped in threes—sizes suitable for Father, Mother, and Baby Bear. One group is selected for immediate use, and the others reserved for future plays.

Spoons may be made by drawing round cardboard

templates, of three different sizes, and cutting out the shapes. If these sets are bound in groups of three with rubber bands, an experience will be gained towards an understanding of multiplication tables, as counts of " one group of three ", " two groups of three ", " three groups of three ", etc., are made.

To the teacher's more earth-bound conventional imagination, the sordid appearance of the Bears' bed-linen leaves something to be desired ! So her next suggestion of pretty patchwork quilts is a very happy one from all points of view, and these are made by pasting coloured shapes on to the newspaper coverlets. Pillows are constructed by pasting the edges of newspaper bags together, then stuffing them with shredded paper, and closing the last edges which were left open for filling purposes.

Number involved.
  Grouping numbers—Bowls and spoons in sets.
  Shapes—Coverlets and pillows.

7. *Father Christmas and his Toy Shop*

Such a seasonal and all-pervading interest as Christmas is rich in possibilities of educational advantage, and our " live " teacher proceeds to frame the programme, and to centre it around this great festival of the Child. Arriving at school one morning, the children see with surprise, that their play-house has been altered almost beyond recognition since school closed the previous afternoon. Then it had been quite an ordinary abode for families of mothers and fathers and their children, now it has been reconditioned and seems to be in possession of a fresh tenant who, to keep out all intruders, has padlocked the front door. Curiosity is still further aroused by the red brick walls, now festooned with icicles, and, on tip-toe with expectation, they eagerly peep through the prettily coloured green, red, and yellow windows. Within the house, a cheerful fire is burning in the grate and ranged round the walls are tables bearing a marvellous array of toys!

" Who is living in our house ? " is the question heard on all sides, and answered almost in the same breath by the children, as they follow the teacher's direction and read over the front door the magic name of " Father Christmas " in large, white letters. It seems incredible that Father Christmas should have come overnight and settled down in their house, but even the most sceptical are convinced as they take another searching look through the windows and see the great man's cloak and hood thrown over the back of a chair, evidently waiting for him.

All doubts dispelled, the children accept the miracle without further inquiry, and their teacher is satisfied that it should be so. For she had once again stayed behind after school hours to serve them (and incidentally her own ends) in setting this scene for the joys of the next day. She had covered the house with icicles, cut from crinkled paper ; filled in the window-panes with coloured cellophane ; lined the inside walls with strips of ceiling paper ; assembled all the children's toys on the tables in the house, with the realistic touch of the uniform on the chair, and finally (before locking the door) had labelled the house with its owner's name! In the dimly-lighted schoolroom, amidst all her preoccupations, inspiration had burned brightly — though it was a dark December afternoon — and opportunities for tapping other interests presented themselves to her imagination. Now these are to be realized during these last days of term, while teacher and children live in and experience the joys of Christmas.

Returning with the little ones to their chairs in the ring, the teacher listens intently to the spontaneous flow of conversation, for this universal favourite is a congenial topic with every child. First one, and then another recalls the surprises brought to their homes on Christmas Eve by the unseen benefactor; then, it is an easy transition in the chatter to the Father Christmas of the toy shop, actually seen by all. Here is the teacher's opening for Father Christmas plays! And so Father Christmas's play-house becomes the toy shop, where all may spend their pennies on the Christmas wares.

The class breaks up into families, and for their accommodation self-contained dwellings are barricaded off by chairs and tables from the adjacent houses — a family to a house. While the children are busy carrying through these domestic arrangements, the teacher quietly dons Father Christmas's uniform (a crimson dressing-gown or kimono with cotton-wool facings), and removes the tables of toys from the play-house placing them outside in a line, or in three sides of a square, whichever is more convenient. For days, the

NUMBER IN THE NURSERY SCHOOL

favourite pastime will be playing Father Christmas and his toy shop, and the teacher should know what are the Number experiences for which these children are ready and be prepared to develop them from the very simple beginnings.

1. The children give coins of any number and value in return for toys. If this is all they are capable of, the teacher will wait until they are ready to go further, for she will realize that so far they have only arrived at an understanding of the principle of barter—giving and getting in return.

2. A further development will be seen when the children try to count the pennies Father Christmas exacts in return for their purchases. The pennies are counted into Father Christmas's hand, and the right understanding of " how many " is shown by the demand for the toy when the correct amount has been tendered.

3. The introduction of price tickets, placed by the goods on the counters, presupposes a still greater advance, for the children calculate and compare before making a purchase.

4. Another development in the play may be made by journeying by 'bus to Father Christmas's shop for this will involve other problems—financial, counting, and grouping. A 'bus, improvised from chairs, may be arranged in two long lines facing each other, or the chairs may be placed in twos ; and the tickets tendered for 'bus journeys will vary according to the time spent in the 'bus.

Number involved.

Counting—Toys, families, chairs for the 'bus.

Grouping—Chairs for the 'bus.

Money—Shopping experiences according to the children's attainments.

Constructive Work : Christmas Decorations.

The familiar chains, simple enough for very little children to make, will naturally suggest counting and comparing of lengths to the children. The number aspect can be stressed, without boredom or tears, by a few simple devices.

The first problem will be to discover the method of making the links, and the teacher should show the children a length of chain already prepared. From this length, the children should cut away one or two links and try to replace them, and, as it is not complicated work, they should be able to make their own discovery of the method. Then, for the teacher, with educational vision, comes the opportunity for combining number and constructive interests. With a certain number of strips, say ten, placed on their tables, the teacher will keep the number aspect before them as they work. One link made, another added on, now only eight strips left on the desk ; five links made, five strips left on the desk. Interest in counting will soon give place to interest in lengths, etc., e.g. " My chain is as long as my table," " My chain is longer than John's," " Mary's chain is not as long as John's," etc. Making chains long enough to reach from window to door will be a possible discovery when several children join their

NUMBER IN THE NURSERY SCHOOL 47

chains together, and the great length will reveal to the children the number of little chains it takes to make such a long one.

Chain-making is an absorbing delight to these little children, and, if it is going to occupy part of the programme—as it may well do—for two or three weeks, the teacher should try to arrange the constructive work so that it furthers number ideas. By arranging the strips in 2's or 3's of different colours, e.g. 2 red, 2 blue, 2 yellow; 3 red, 3 blue, 3 yellow, etc., interest in group arrangements will result.

> *Number involved.*
> *Counting*—Links, strips, lengths.
> *Adding and subtracting.*
> *Measurement*—Grouping.

II. RHYTHMIC INTERESTS

It is striking to see how largely Number features in the traditional rhymes and games, and the good teacher will seek to make her collection of these as all-embracing as possible. The number may be emphasized quite legitimately, provided that the game itself does not suffer.

Some of the games can be played *en masse* with large classes; but others should be used for groups only, the groups playing with speed, for the repetition with successive groups will help to strengthen the number associations. The two experiences of actually participating in the game and of watching others, tend especially towards this end.

NUMBER IN THE NURSERY SCHOOL

| *Games and Method of Playing.* | *Number Involved.* |

1. *Rhymes.*

(i) " This little pig went to market,
　　This little pig stayed at home,
　　This little pig ate the roast beef,
　　This little pig had none,
　　And this little pig cried
　　　' Week, week, week,' all the way home."

　　Although a very simple play it gives the children an idea of *analysing* a whole into smaller parts.

　This is played with the fingers; each finger in turn taking the part of a pig.

(ii) " There were two birds sat on a stone,
　　Fa, la, la, la, lal, de;
　　One flew away and then there was one,
　　Fa, la, la, la, lal, de;
　　The other flew after and then there was none,
　　Fa, la, la, la, lal, de;
　　And so the poor stone was left alone,
　　Fa, la, la, la, lal, de."

　　First ideas of *subtraction*.

　The two forefingers are placed on the table, and mark time to the words of the first line as they are recited by the teacher or children. At the third line, one flies away, leaving one, and at the fifth line the other flies away, leaving none.

(iii)　　" Here is the beehive,
　　　Where are the bees?
　Hid in the way where nobody sees,
　Here they come creeping out of the hive—
　One, two, three, four, five."

　　Counting.

　The children hold their closed fists during the recital of the first three

NUMBER IN THE NURSERY SCHOOL 49

Games and Method of Playing.	Number Involved.
lines, and release the bees (the fingers) as the numbers are repeated. The bees fly round and finally return to the hive.	
(iv) " 1, 2 — Buckle my shoe. 3, 4 — Shut the door. 5, 6 — Pick up sticks. 7, 8 — Lay them straight. 9, 10 — A good fat hen."	*Counting* numbers to 10. *Grouping* numbers in twos.

As the numbers are recited they should be shown by holding up the corresponding number of fingers. The intermediate lines can be put to appropriate actions, e.g. the children may pretend to buckle their shoes.

(v) " The Christmas Pudding."

| " 1, 2 — How do you do?
3, 4 — Sit on the floor.
5, 6 — I've a pudding to mix.
7, 8 — So I mustn't be late.
9, 10 — Here's a helping for Ben.
11, 12 — Fork and delve.
13, 14 — Please stop talking.
15, 16 — Eggs a'whisking.
17, 18 — Don't mind waiting.
19, 20 — We'll all have plenty." | *Counting* numbers to 20.
Grouping numbers in twos. |

The children stand in pairs, facing each other. As the numbers are recited, they should be shown by holding up the corresponding number of fingers ; one child of each pair dealing with the odd numbers while her partner responds with the even.

The intermediate lines can be put to appropriate actions, e.g. the children may bow, sit on the floor, mix the pudding, etc.

NUMBER IN THE NURSERY SCHOOL

Games and Method of Playing.	*Number Involved.*

(vi) " Ten little Nigger Boys."

Ten children are chosen to stand in a row. They must be counted before the game begins for the sake of accuracy. The teacher repeats the rhyme and the children join in if they wish to. As tragedy overtakes each little nigger, he sits on the floor or runs back to his seat, and those left are counted each time.

Counting up to ten and from ten downwards.

Subtracting. Idea given as each little boy is taken away. The teacher will make some spontaneous comment on the reduced number, laying emphasis on the number now reached.

(vii) " I love sixpence, pretty little sixpence,
  I love sixpence better than my life.
   I spent a penny of it,
   I kept a penny of it,
   I took fourpence home to my wife.
  " I love fourpence, pretty little fourpence,
   I love fourpence better than my life.
   I spent a penny of it,
   I kept a penny of it,
   I took twopence home to my wife.
  " I love twopence, pretty little twopence,
   I love twopence better than my life.
   I spent a penny of it,
   I kept a penny of it,
   I took nothing home to my wife."

The children are provided with an envelope containing a (cardboard) silver sixpence and six pennies.

The game is introduced by the

Counting.
Subtraction in twos.

NUMBER IN THE NURSERY SCHOOL 51

Games and Method of Playing.	*Number Involved.*
teacher giving its title while the children put their silver sixpence on the desk.	
This is then changed into six pennies, and as each verse is said so the amount lost is returned to the envelope.	

2. *Group Games.*

(i) " Soldier Boy."

"Soldier boy, soldier boy, where are you going,
Bearing so bravely the red, white, and blue ?
I'm doing my duty, and helping my country,
If you'll be a soldier boy, you may come too."

Addition and Subtraction. The teacher will help the children to realize the increase in the soldier boy's line, and the decreases in the onlookers' two lines.

The children stand or sit in two lines facing each other. The soldier boy, bearing a Union Jack, marches up and down between the lines. During the singing of the last line he stands in front of a child (his choice) to whom he hands the flag. The child chosen joins the soldier boy and becomes leader.

(ii) " Oranges and Lemons."
(iii) " Nuts and May."

These need no description, though a word of advice is offered on methods of keeping alive the number interest.

Adding and Subtracting. The teacher should call for many recounts of sides.

In *Oranges and Lemons* the whole verse should only be sung through once, then the chop, chop, and choosing of fruit should follow.

Weight. Through the tug-of-war in Oranges and Lemons and " fetching away " in Nuts and May, the children should begin to try to account for

NUMBER IN THE NURSERY SCHOOL

Games and Method of Playing.	*Number Involved.*
	the losses and gains, when they see the sides very unequally matched.
3. *Marching Games.*	
Marching 5, 10, or any number of big, little, tiny steps.	*Counting* and *judging* amounts or degrees.
Stamping, hopping, tiptoeing in numbered steps as above.	
Crossing a room in 10, 15, 20, 30 steps.	*Counting.*
4. *Games for the Ears.*	
So many claps, whistles, strikes of a push-bell.	*Counting.*
Strikes of a triangle, etc., in soft, loud, medium, two or three of each or in any pattern.	*Grouping,* e.g.— 3 soft, 3 loud, etc.
5. *Games for the Eyes.*	
Surprise bags or small baskets of conkers, acorns, or nuts are unpacked while children watch and count, one child at a time coming out to take one or a group of 3, 5, etc.	*Counting and Grouping.* In the re-packing it should be ascertained that the original number has been returned. In grouping, the teacher should try to bring the idea of " times " to the children's consciousness. e.g. " Jenny has *one* group of 3, put them back in the bag, Jenny. Now Ronny's group of 3. Jenny's and Ronny's groups have gone into the bag. " So *two* groups of three have gone back to the bag."

NUMBER IN THE NURSERY SCHOOL 53

III. NUMBER WORK OF A MORE ABSTRACT NATURE

Individual occupations have usually catered for this formal type of work, rather than for the play, constructive and rhythmic interests dealt with in the first part of this chapter. The over-emphasis laid on these individual occupations has caused them to become anathema to those progressive teachers, to whom experience is the be-all and end-all of number teaching. But it is a mistake to rule them out of the Nursery School altogether, for there is no doubt that some children can deal with formal Number at an earlier stage than others. The abstract appeals to them and they delight in number for number's sake. Pat, at $4\frac{1}{2}$, spent much time in his father's library arranging sets of books in numerical order because he loved " awanging books in a sewies ".

If, then, individual occupations appeal to the children and suggest ideas to them, they have a legitimate part to play in helping to further the little ones' mathematical concepts. Not only so, they strengthen the power of memory to accumulate, as the children " pick up " useful number facts and store them away for future need.

Suggestions for Individual Occupations suitable for the Nursery School

1. *Arranging Papers of Different Colours and Lengths.*

A packet of coloured poster papers mounted on cardboard, cut into different lengths is given to the children to arrange in any ways they like. Arrangement may be according to colours, lengths; or the children may make them into patterns, which will help to give them experience in fitting means to an end.

(*a*) According to colours.

(*b*) According to lengths.

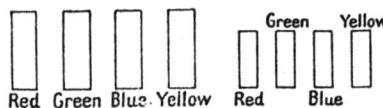

(*c*) Making patterns.

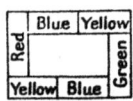

(*d*) Making stairs.

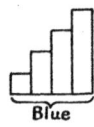

2. *Arranging Shapes of Different Colours and Sizes.*

In the same way a packet of shapes will give children opportunities for comparison of shape, size, pattern-making.

NUMBER IN THE NURSERY SCHOOL 55

(a) According to colours.

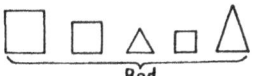

(b) According to size and shape.

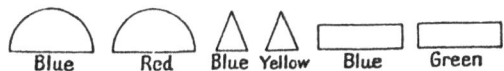

(c) Making patterns.

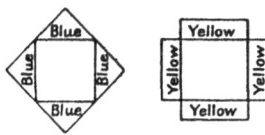

3. *Dominoes.*

Only the simplest form of this game is possible for most children up to 5 years of age.

It is wiser for the teacher to make her own dominoes, printing on the number groups with a pencil-end dipped into poster paint, on whole or half post cards. The small domino sets of the toy shop are very confusing.

4. *A packet of pictures with number symbols* for the children to place by the side.

With a small printing outfit the teacher can rapidly make numbers of these cards.

56 NUMBER IN THE NURSERY SCHOOL

5. *Numbering the Houses in our Street.*

A packet of post cards, on each of which is drawn a house, and a packet of numbers to place on the front doors of the houses, will be a meaningful occupation for the tinies.

6. *Pairs.*

Pairs of gloves, shoes, etc., are pasted on strips of paper with a wide space between each pair. These are numbered from an envelope containing symbols of the even numbers.

7. *Odd and Even.*

Two strips of pictures, with symbols to attach, are arranged—

As odd numbers.

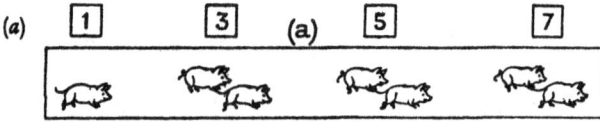

As even numbers.

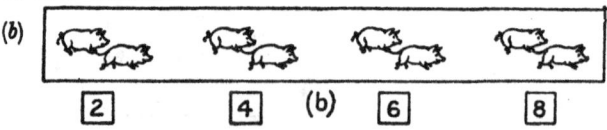

8. *Number Groups and Symbols.*

Two packets of cards to be arranged in sequence with corresponding symbols by the side.

9. *Tram Tickets and Money.*

The children are provided with tram tickets of different values, and a packet of cardboard money.

The tickets are placed on the table or floor, and the right number of pennies placed on each ticket.

10. *" Paper " Shops.*

A packet of pictures of goods bought in shops, together with cardboard pennies, can be treated as above.

These are only a few suggestions for Number experiences in the Baby Room. The ingenious teacher, whose main interest is in children, will naturally be able to add to or make her own lists. Before concluding this chapter, it might be helpful to give some suggestions to those teachers who are attached to Nursery Classes where (unfortunately, much to our shame) the fixed time table is considered of more importance than the children, and definite Number lessons have to be given each day.

1. The programme must be planned with regard to variety; some activities catering for the whole class can be taken, and followed by group and individual work.

2. Activities must appeal to the children's instinctive interests, and be varied, e.g. (a) muscular activities involving legs, throat, eye, or ear should form part of the programme; (b) constructive activities; (c) play interests.

Two Sample Programmes, Taken from Students' Notebooks

I. *Apparatus*—Push-bell, boxes of beads, strings of three lengths for each child.

(1) Marching games for counting. These will be taken with the whole class, marching five big stamps,

Standing still for five claps,

Five little steps, etc.

(2) Listening games for counting. Children will cover eyes and count while the push-bell is struck, say, eight times.

(3) Group games—for adding and subtracting.

Ten Little Nigger Boys.

Oranges and Lemons.

Three groups of six children in each group will be the Oranges and Lemons. (If the children wish to continue, we shall play again, but the children will probably want a change after the game has been played two or three times.)

(4) Constructive work—for counting and measuring.

Children will have the boxes of paper beads they have been making in class and will make—

(i) A necklace.
(ii) A bracelet.
(iii) A long chain.

Strings of different lengths will be placed on the teacher's table and the children will come out and choose for themselves the one they judge is best fitted for the task they have set themselves.

II. *Apparatus*—Envelopes containing 6*d*. and six pennies.
Bundles of tram tickets.
Shopping cards. Strips of paper. Pencils.

NUMBER IN THE NURSERY SCHOOL   59

1. *Soldier Boy.*

This game will be taken as an introduction to the lesson so as to give the children some muscular activity.

2. *I Love Sixpence.*

The whole class will play this game. It will give exercise for hand and throat. Children will count, and subtract in this game, they will also be helped to understand the equal value of the sixpence and sixpennies.

3. *Group and Individual Work.*

(a) 'Bus play with groups.

The teacher will play the 'bus game with eight or so children at a time. As the children have played this game several times before, a development in the play will be attempted to-day.

The 'bus will stop at 1*d*., 2*d*., 3*d*. stage ; the 1*d*. ride will be a short one, the 2*d*. longer, and the 3*d*. longest of all.

(b) Shopping cards or tram tickets. Individual work.

The children will use their envelopes containing the 6*d*. They will put the right number of coins on the tram tickets or shopping cards.

Chapter III

NUMBER ARISING FROM PROJECTS

> "What is needed is a new orientation of school instruction which shall bring it into closer correlation with the natural movements of children's minds."—*The Primary Report.*

Those educationists who have long recognized this as their urgent need welcome the 1933 Infant and Nursery School Report; and, as they seek new bearings find their justification and direction in this one pregnant sentence: " During the infant stage the play-way is the best way " (p. 125). The children who are " learning to live in a changing world ", must be afforded experiences arising out of their own interests, for it is by such experiences they learn. Further, the only sure guides to the character and manner of their learning are their interests; therefore, " The curriculum is to be thought of in terms of activity and experience, rather than of knowledge to be acquired and facts to be stored " (p. 122). The haphazard experiences of childhood, " the seemingly unordered ways " are at an early period associated with efforts at rationalizing, and these bring about gradually an order and a system. Though the child in the infant school has not yet reached a stage in which intellectual discipline has to be maintained by making the various branches of knowledge the subject

NUMBER ARISING FROM PROJECTS 61

of special study, it pursues activities and interests, has experience, and tries experiments; but subjects, *as such*, do not come within his scope. Here we have the psychology of the Project method put into a nutshell. The complete justification of a project lies in the fact that it originates in the children's interests; and if it develops on sound lines the need for subjects will be felt, or as Professor Findlay has it, we " get at subjects ". And "learning takes place",[1] as purposeful activities are carried forward, though it must be clearly recognized that a project only undertakes to motivate subjects. Here we venture to join issue with the Report in respect of the entire banishment of subjects from the Infant School, and more especially with regard to Number. For the Number experiences described in this chapter can, in most cases, be followed by definite Number lessons and systematic schemes. It will be found that the Number processes thus motivated demand reasoning, and would be better dealt with in the "oral lesson" which "has still a definite place in the school procedure".[2] The children's needs actually furnish the occasion for such lessons, and, as the Report goes on to say, " However wide may be the range of attainment between the most and least advanced members of the class, there will always be some sufficiently level in attainment to be treated as a group—and many concrete problems—can also be studied or at any rate started best in class."[3]

In this chapter examples are taken from my student's

[1] Dewey, *Democracy and Education*, p. 161.
[2] *Infant and Nursery Schools*, p. 144. [3] Ibid.

notebooks. The following projects have been worked in the large classes of the elementary schools, with children from 5½ to 7 years. (Only the Number work involved in these projects is dealt with here.) The reader is again reminded that a project only undertakes to *motivate* subjects, and these Number experiences were in most cases followed by definite Number lessons and systematic schemes.

I. SHOPS

The tendency among all children is to imitate the activities of their surroundings, and shops and shopping constantly become the focus of interest for town children.

As almost everything required for the shops can be made in the handwork periods, the heavy task of preparing material is considerably lightened by the children's contributions. Collecting and hoarding match, boot, and other boxes, newspapers, bottles, and waste materials of all descriptions, are eagerly and almost passionately undertaken by the would-be shopkeepers. As the " dump " grows apace, inspiration follows, and teachers and children find that they can compete with the factory for speed in turning out the finished article. But, from the teacher's point of view, the work becomes more difficult and calls for careful organizing as the shop play begins. For the twofold aim of the teacher's and the children's purpose must be constantly borne in mind. The children, in recapitulating life situations, *must play* ; the teacher, as guide

NUMBER ARISING FROM PROJECTS 63

and educationist, *must regulate the experiences* using them as vantage-points from which the interest may be urged forward. Not the least of the difficulties is the fact that classrooms are not designed for the activities of fifty or more bustling shopkeepers and their patrons. Most teachers find it impossible to have all the children out of their places at one time and compromise accordingly in different ways. The following suggestions are offered from experience gained in practice in large classes of the Elementary Schools.

1. *Shopping and Handwork Activities Carried on Simultaneously*

A group of eight or ten children may be engaged in shopping-play, buying and selling furiously; the teacher should devote her attention mainly to this group, for she must watch and help, looking out for incidental opportunities to be followed later, either with individual, group, or class lessons, according to the need for such instruction in the individual, group, or whole class. The remainder of the class should continue with the factory work; and, as they produce more stock for the shops, they will face again, and now independently, the constructive problems of the handwork periods.

2. *Free and Directed Shopping*

At other times the class can be divided into two groups for shopping.

(a) *Free Play in the Shop.*—A small group of eight or ten children can play with only the teacher's eye upon them now and then, the play will be the thing, and the teacher should only step in if there are disputes urgently in need of settlement.

(b) *Directed Shopping.*—This group consists of all the children, who are ready for definite teaching, and for a consolidation of their experiences, if the shopping is to continue to be of any value to them.

A large shop front is made from a brown paper framework with pockets, into which the goods for sale fit, and in such a way that the greater part of them is seen above the pocket. These goods are coloured, cut out in stiff cartridge paper, and priced. Each child has an envelope containing similar cut-outs and a pile of coins. The teacher acts as shopkeeper and sells one or more goods (according to whether the process required is addition or subtraction) to the children, who are called out to choose from the shop front. The rest of the class take the corresponding goods from their envelopes, place them on their desks with the correct number of coins by the side, and either add amounts, or find the right change from a coin, or even work in both processes as the case may be.

It is important to stress the following points with regard to the Number work involved in buying and selling :—

(i) *A Progressive Scheme must be Worked out.*

At first the idea of barter must be gained, and all that the youngest children should be expected to grasp, is that money must be given in return for goods. At this stage (about four to five years) the " how much "

NUMBER ARISING FROM PROJECTS 65

will not concern them. Later, the right amount of money must be given for purchases, and the prices affixed should be such that the children are able to deal with them, e.g. shopping will be with sixpences, shillings, and ten shilling treasury notes.

Following on from this stage will come the purchase of two or more goods, the making of bills and later still there will be the giving and receiving of change.

With the gain of experience and confidence, the shopping should involve more complicated processes, e.g. making bills with addition and subtraction, or purchasing and giving change ; multiplication, addition and subtraction in " bills and parcels ".

(ii) *Group and Class Lessons will be Necessary.*

When the children begin to find themselves in difficulties and the teacher realizes that the play is not worth while, she must see to it that more knowledge is acquired if the interest is not to pass into futility but to keep its educational value. The stores should be closed, and the storekeepers and shoppers gathered together for one or more group or class lessons, in which the concrete material of the money can be used to solve the problems created through the experience.

(iii) *Bills.*

These should also be dealt with in a progressive order.

(a) A simple form of bill, merely a pictorial representation of the purchase with the correct number of pennies drawn up by the side, makes a good introduction to an understanding of bills, e.g. a string of beads and six pennies.

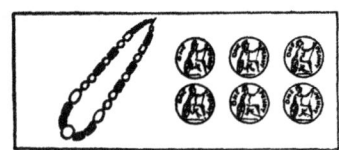

(b) A column for pence, with a guiding line for the placing of the purchase, which may at first be represented by drawing and later by writing, will be the beginning of work with bills proper.

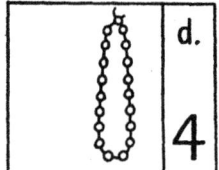 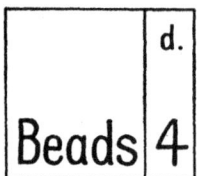

(c) Addition in bills.

(d) Subtraction.

(c)

1	Doll	s.	d. 6
2	Pencils		2
1	Ship		3
			11

(d)

I have	s. 1	d. 0
I spend		3
Change		9

(iv) *Number work involved in Shopping Experiences.*

Shopping Must be True to Life.—In each shop, trade methods must be carefully followed and the transactions carried through as in real life, though prices may

NUMBER ARISING FROM PROJECTS 67

be adapted to suit the stage of development and educational needs of the customers.

(a) *The Sweet Shop*—Sweets are sold by :—
"So many"; length—bars, half-bars; boxes; weight—ounce, 2 oz., ¼, ½, and 1 lb.

(b) *Greengrocer.*
"So many," e.g. oranges.
Dozen, e.g. bananas, oranges.
Weight, 1 lb., ½, ¼, ¾ lb.
Dry Measure, pint, quart, peck, bushel, bag, sack.

(c) *Grocer.* Tins or packets.
Weight, 1 lb., ½, ¼, ¾ lb.

(d) *Draper.* Linear Measure.
Materials, by the yard, ½, ¼, ¾ yard.
Ribbon widths by the inch.
Buttons, by the dozen, half, quarter, three-quarter ; and Pins by the ½, ¼ lb., in ones.

(e) *Stationery.*
Writing-paper by the packet.
Envelopes by the packet, 12, 20, 25.
Plain Post Cards by the 6, 11, 12, 25.
Picture Cards singly.

(f) *Dairy.*
Wet Measure : Quart, pint, ½, ¼ pint.
Cartons—Cream Ices.
Weight : 1 lb., ½, ¼, ¾ lb. Butter.
Weight : 1 lb., ½, ¼, ¾ lb. ; Sections : fractions—one-sixth, one-eighth. Cheeses.

(g) *House Decorators'.*
Wallpaper by the piece, i.e. 12 yards (" doll's yard ").
Friezes, borders by the yard.

(h) *Furnishing Shop.*
Materials by the yard.
Down, hair for stuffing by the 1 lb.
Treasury notes will be required.

Sales.—These should be arranged as in life. The articles may be reduced by so much in the shilling, or everything marked half-price. From several points of view, sales and Christmas bazaars can be joyous occasions at the end of term, as all the stock can be cleared leaving the room in readiness for the cleaners.

SHOPS

Goods.	Methods of Procuring.	Number in Handwork.
1. *Toy Shop.* Engines, 'Buses, Aeroplanes, Boats, Ships, Motor Cars, Vehicles of all sorts.	Waste material, e.g. matchboxes, boot-boxes, milk-bottle tops, paints.	These are all made as isolated toys bearing no relation to each other, and as co-operation is not attempted in the making, no common unit of measure is used.
Dolls.	(1) Made from stockings stuffed with shredded newspaper, or, (2) Newspaper rolled into cylindrical shapes with a painted mask for the face and crinkled paper for dresses and bonnets. These make excellent dolls.	Proportions in the toy itself are looked for, and the children's attention is directed to the various parts with the aim of leading them on to a better understanding of measurement and scale, later.
Dolls' Houses.	Cardboard cartons for houses, match boxes for furniture, pegs dressed in crinkled paper for the occupants.	
Kites.	Two sticks 12 by 16 inches tied at right angles. Sheets of sugar, pastel, and coloured tissue paper. 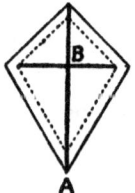	*Measurement* taken and two sticks chosen in correct proportion. Framework measured on paper. Getting the right *length* for the tail because of balance in flying.

NUMBER ARISING FROM PROJECTS

Goods.	Methods of Procuring.	Number involved in Constructive Work.
	The tied framework is laid on sugar or pastel paper, and lines drawn from point to point. The outside edge should be 1 to 1½ inches wider. A string, the same length as the vertical stick, is tied to the stick at A. The tail is made from twisted tissue paper tied at intervals.	
Reins. Skipping Ropes.	Plaited raffia or thick rug wool made into chains by the knotting stitch.	*Length.* The test is: " Are my reins long enough for driving; my rope for skipping ? "

2. *Jeweller's Shop.*

Rings, Necklaces, Pendants.	(1) Sticks of macaroni broken into lengths. Coloured with watercolour or poster paint. (2) Beads modelled in clay and pierced with a knitting needle to make the hole, and left to dry on the needle. When dry, they are painted and finally varnished.	*Counting, Measuring.* Arranging beads in two's, three's, etc.; or in sizes ranging from the largest bead in the centre to the smallest bead at each end.
Jewel Cases.	Covered with wallpapers, lined with soft tissue folded to fit, or with cotton wool.	*Measuring.* The measuring experiences described in similar examples in the last chapter, are the foundation for the children's use of the unit of measure. The covering paper for the boxes is cut to the correct widths, and the child's problem is to deal with lengths of paper in relation to the length of sides of boxes.

Goods.	Methods of Procuring.	Number involved in Constructive Work.
Clocks.	Circular cheese boxes covered with a face of white paper, fastened on to a base of a rectangular box.	*Figure Writing.* N.B. Younger children will use Arabic figures, and the older ones the Roman.
Watches.	Small circles of paper. The finished watch can be pasted on to a band of ribbon for a wristlet watch.	*Learning to tell the Time.* *Figure Writing* and time as above. *Measurement* for wrists (with a piece of string). Another problem is to fix the watch in the centre of the ribbon.

3. *Sweet Shop.*

Toffees. Boiled Sweets. Peppermint Creams, Chocolates. Arranged in boxes covered with wallpaper.	Newspapers covered with crinkled papers. Plasticine, or clay painted when dry.	Arranged to be sold at " so many " for 1d. *Multiplication tables.* Arrangement in boxes in lines 4, 6, 8.
Bars of Rock.	Lengths of paper about 2 by 12 inches painted with a wash of pale crimson lake and when dry rolled into a long tube. Half and quarter bars can be found by folding and cutting the paper before painting.	Sweets sold by the *length*, e.g. rock and chocolate sticks may be measured by a unit of measure given to the children, or with the foot rule.
Sticks of Chocolate.	(1) Clay. (2) Strip wood, measured into lengths—w h o l e, half, and quarter-bar—covered with silver paper.	*Length.* *Fractions.*

4. *Greengrocer's.*

Fruits. Apples, Oranges, Bananas,	(1) Clay modelling. The fruit may be made full	*Solids, Shapes.* *Comparison of Sizes.*

NUMBER ARISING FROM PROJECTS

Goods.	Methods of Procuring.	Number involved in Constructive Work.
Grape Fruit, Grape.	size by comparison with the real fruit. If this is precluded by the enormous amount of clay required for a large class, a lump, about the real size, should be given to the children, who are told they are going to make four smaller fruits from it. After some experiments they should be able to discover that the best plan is to halve and then quarter their clay.	*Fractions*, half and quarter.
Vegetables. Celery, Cabbages, Brussels Sprouts, Rhubarb,	Crinkled paper cut and folded to the required shape. (Crinkled paper is recommended because it takes water colour.)	*Measurement.*
Potatoes.	Newspaper balls covered with brown paper.	

5. *Grocer's Shop.*

Dummy Packets and tins of Cereals, Cocoa, Tea, Coffee, Sugar.	(1) These are usually collected by the children. (2) A very keen teacher could give the children plans of the packets, putting before them the problem of cutting out and discovering how to fit together to construct the required packet. The packets can be filled with sand, flour, dried peas, lentils, rice, etc.	Different *sizes* and comparison of *weights*. Introduction to *plan-making*. *Solids.*

6. *The Dairy.*

Milk and Cream.	Starch or whitening mixed thick or thin for cream or milk, and measured out into bottles and cartons.	*Wet Measure.* Quart, pint, half-pint. Cartons of pint, half, and quarter-pint.

NUMBER IN THE INFANT SCHOOL

Goods.	Methods of Procuring.	Number involved in Constructive Work.
Butter.	Clay modelling with butter-pats. The finished shape should be painted, if possible, with poster paint, failing that with water colour.	*Weight.* Pound, half, and quarter-pound.
Cheese.	Clay modelling. The clay is pressed into the round boxes and cut in sections, half, quarter, third, sixth, and left to dry before being painted.	*Fractions.* Wholing and parting into fractions.

7. *Stationers'.*
   Stationery :

(*a*) Writing Paper	Paper cut to a certain width is given out, for the children to measure the lengths of the sheets of paper and to fold in half.	*Grouping.* Packets of paper, in dozens or half-dozens.
(*b*) Envelopes.	Constructed from a rectangle of paper, to fit the folded sheets.	*Measurement.* Using foot rules, or by folding only. *Plan making.* *Grouping.* As for writing paper.

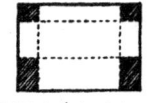

Corners cut away.

(*c*) Post cards.	Cut from cartridge paper. The width at the back is halved and spaced for correspondence and addresses.	*Measurement.*—Length of post cards is given, and the children measure the width. *Grouping.* Postcards are made up into sixes, dozens, or elevens.
(*d*) Birthday and Christmas Cards.	These may be of various shapes, folded or flat.	*Measurement.*
Calendars.	In writing lessons, days, months, and year can be dealt with or the sheets may be hectographed	*Counting and figure writing* up to 31 for the first three or four months. For the

NUMBER ARISING FROM PROJECTS

Goods.	Methods of Procuring.	Number involved in Constructive Work.
	for the children to fill in dates. The months ruled out in spaces for dates.	remainder of the year, the first of each month should be found, and the children encouraged to find the dates a week, a fortnight, and three weeks later by adding on in sevens.

Experiences in working to scale: A strip of paper, *The Doll's Yard*, 9 inches to the yard, is pinned on to the children's desks, this equals " 1 doll's yard ".

8. *Drapery.*

Bales of plain and printed materials from wall paper or kitchen paper.	Widths of wall or kitchen paper are given to the children, and these are measured off into so many "doll's yards," before being wound on to rectangular pieces of cardboard for bales. As the fractions of the yard are required, they are dealt with by folding the paper measure.	*Measurement and Fractions.* $\frac{1}{2}, \frac{1}{4}, \frac{3}{4}$ of the "doll's yard" are found by folding.
Ribbons from wall or kitchen paper.	As above.	
Lace.	Strips of paper are folded, the edges rounded or cut into points. Lace-work is represented by "surprise" paper-cutting, i.e. by cutting shapes in the folded paper.	
Pattern books and Patterns.	The provision of manufacturer's materials would be too expensive for school work. As only paper is used for the bales, the sensory-experiences of touch so necessary for infant-school children may be	*Shapes* Learning to write prices, e.g. 1s. per yard, 6d. per yard.

74 NUMBER IN THE INFANT SCHOOL

Goods.	Methods of Procuring.	Number involved in Constructive Work.
	supplied by compiling pattern books from the materials of various textures found in the rag-bag, e.g. silk, cotton, velvet, flannel, etc. These are cut into appropriate shapes, pasted in books, and priced.	
Buttons.	Cards of buttons may be made by sewing buttons on to thin cardboard. Or, button-moulds may be used as templates for the children to draw round and colour.	*Grouping.* Cards should be divided lengthways in half and again widthways into quarters. The buttons should be arranged in 2's, 4's, 6's, or 8's in these four divisions.
Dress Department. Dresses for Dolls.	As paper dolls will be the most suitable customers for a shop where paper clothing is sold, jointed dolls from Dennison's, Kingsway, can be provided. Paper frocks for these may be constructed and sold in the dress department.	*Scale*: The Doll's Yard will be used for measuring. *N.B.*—It is important that the "doll's yard" is always called by the whole name. It should never be compared or related to the foot measure, though it may be compared with the yard.
Millinery Department. Paper Hats.	(1) A circle of paper, with a triangular segment cut away and joined at the edges A, B, C, then trimmed with paper flowers and ribbons, makes a pretty hat.	*Circles and their construction.* Children should use compasses if possible.

NUMBER ARISING FROM PROJECTS

Goods.	Methods of Procuring.	Number involved in Constructive Work.
	(2) A circle of thin cardboard with a small concentric circle cut away. Through this is pushed a larger circular piece of tissue paper which is arranged to form a crown, while the inner edges are pasted to the back of the inner circle. A lining is pasted on both sides of the cardboard circle to cover the cardboard.	Circles and concentric circles.

| Sunbonnets. | A circle of soft paper and a half-circle of thin cardboard. | Circles. Half-circles. |

The soft paper is pasted over the half circle and shaped to form the back of the bonnet.

10. *House Decorator's.*

| Wallpaper. | Widths of paper are given to the children and cut off into lengths of a dozen "doll's yards", to make the piece | Scale: 9 inches = "doll's yard". |
| Friezes. | Lengths are given to the children, these are measured off by the "doll's yard." | N.B.—In the wallpaper shop, further measuring experiences may be given in |

76 NUMBER IN THE INFANT SCHOOL

Goods.	Methods of Procuring.	Number involved in Constructive Work.
Pattern books.	Rectangles are cut from remnants left from lengths of wallpaper and friezes. As these have to fit in a book of patterns, they must all be made to the same size.	spacing of designs, but care is needed not to labour this work so that the children's interest does not flag.

11. *Furniture Shop.*

Chairs, Tables, Chesterfields, Chests of Drawers, Cupboards, etc.	(a) From waste material, or (b) Cutting out pictures from catalogues and mounting them on stiff cartridge paper.	*Ideas of Proportion.*
Carpets.	Weaving on cardboard looms which must be warped for the children.	(a) *Measurement.* The woof can be cut in strands of the width of the cardboard frame. (b) Grouping of strands, e.g. 12 red, 3 blue; or (c) by measurement, e.g. 2 inches red, 1 inch blue, 6 inches green, etc.
Linoleums.	Patterns of herring-boning, or square designs are made with brown-paper squares and rectangles which are pasted on to a background of paper, e.g. :—	*Measurement.* Squares and oblongs measured and cut out and arranged for patterns.

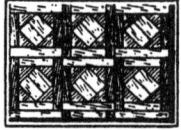
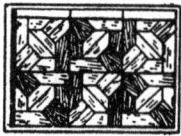

NUMBER ARISING FROM PROJECTS 77

II. 'BUSES

It is only possible really to play this game with a small group, as of all the plays it is the most difficult to carry through in a large class. About ten or twelve children can form the group and the rest of the class should be provided with other occupations such as play with toys, drawing, or they may arrange the 'bus tickets in packets.

The arrangement of the 'bus is carried out according to the children's knowledge of omnibus services. The conductor's booth is marked by a chalk line on the floor, and the driver's seat is just behind the engine —an inverted soap box. Each passenger has a number of pennies, and the only other equipment needed is a conductor's ticket outfit with punch complete, a push bell, a whistle, and a cardboard clock. It is as well for the teacher at first to take the part of conductor, so that she may " keep the pot boiling " by infusing fun, life, and reality into the game. The driver's seat is filled by one of the children.

As the conductor places the clock hands at say 9 or 10 o'clock he announces that the 'bus will start at that hour, the children then take their seats.

Goods.	Methods of Procuring.	Number involved.
Tickets.	Paper, coloured and numbered according to the regulations of the London Transport Board. (b) Children may collect tickets and supplement numbers as above.	*Figure Writing, Multiplication and Division.* Counting and arranging tickets in dozens according to values. Giving change. Ideas of distance in journeys of different lengths.

G

78 NUMBER IN THE INFANT SCHOOL

Goods.	Methods of Procuring.	Number Involved.
Time Tables and Clocks.	Paper.	Time. Starting of buses.
'Bus Maps.	Collected by the children and used for observation if the children are interested in and can appreciate the map.	Beginnings of understanding of plans and map reading.

III. FESTIVALS, E.G. CHRISTMAS

Constructive Work.	Method.	Number in Constructive Work.
Chains	The children may measure and cut their own chains.	*Measurement* by strip units, or by foot-ruler according to age and experience of children. *Multiplication and Division*, idea of " times ". *Arrangement* in two's, three's, etc.
Icicles	White crinkled paper cut into icicles of different lengths.	*Measurement.* Fitting the strips into given spaces on walls, teacher's desk, etc.
Crackers.	Crinkled paper. 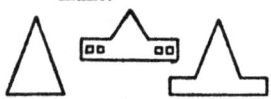	*Measurement*, getting proportions for wrapping present in cracker.
Caps for Crackers.	Coloured tissues. Several shapes are shown to children; and they choose which they will make.	*Measurement.* The head is measured with tape, or tape measure, and the caps made from these. Further measurement may be given in decorating with motifs. *Division.* Arranging crackers in boxes.
Presents, e.g. Cards, Calendars, Blotters, etc.	Cardboard, paper.	*Measurement.* See section on Stationer's Shop.

IV. Lunch or Party Equipment

Materials.	Methods of Procuring.	Number involved in Constructive Work.
Plates.	Cartridge paper plates decorated with motifs.	Circles and their properties are discovered with (a) templates or (b) compasses, according to children's age. Spacing of motifs will give further measuring experiences. *Division.* In making into packets of 6 or 12.
Table cloths.	Kitchen paper or wall paper.	*Measurement and Addition.* The table is measured and an additional piece allowed for flaps.
Cups.	Decorated cream cartons with handles of paper.	*Measurement* in handles, and spacing of motifs.
Saucers.	Cheese boxes decorated.	*Measurement,* spacing and arrangement of motifs.
Table Napkins.	Coloured tissue papers.	*Measurement. Division,* making into packets, so many in a packet.

V. The Zoo

The animals may be given to the children, or they may model them from plasticine, or draw and cut them out. If the children construct them, they will have constant recourse to them for comparison in considering shelters and their other requirements.

Constructive Work.	Method.	Number involved.
Shelters.	Boxes chosen in relation to height and length of animals.	*Rough Measurement.*
Bars for Cages.	Cane, skewers, strips of wood.	*Lengths* measured in relation to boxes.

Constructive Work.	Method.	Number involved.
		Widths between bars must be measured to ensure even distribution of bars and prevent escape of animals.
Doors of Cages.		Cut in relation to *height* of animals.
Grounds of Zoo.	Paper—brown strips for paths. Green rectangles for grass, brown shapes for flower-beds.	As in gardens for houses and farms. (See Chapter II.)
Tickets.	Thin cardboard or cartridge paper.	*Measurement.* Two strips to be used as units of measurement for length and breadth. *Arranged* in dozens. Adults and children, half-price for children.
Armlets for Keepers.	Brown paper strips.	*Measured* with tape, or tape-measure on keeper's arm.
Clocks for opening and closing times.	Paper. (See Chapter VI on 12 as measuring unit.)	*Time.*
Money for admission and buying food at food stalls.	Brown and white paper. Coins used as templates.	*Money.* Giving change. Totalling day's takings.
Food for Animals.	Plasticine, clay, or dough mixture.	*Grouping*—made up into packets of a dozen, half, quarter dozen, or sold by weight. One pound, half, quarter pound.

VI. THE STREET

The street may be a strip of wallpaper stretched across the front of the classroom, or a space may be marked off on the floor.

NUMBER ARISING FROM PROJECTS

Constructive Work.	*Method.*	*Number in Constructive Work.*
Houses and Shops.		
(a) Buildings.	Houses will be drawn by the children on a background of cartridge paper. This will form one side of the street. For the opposite side, buildings may be constructed from (i) waste materials—boxes, or (ii) from large envelopes on to which has been pasted a covering for the front and two flaps to act as stands, as in illustration. 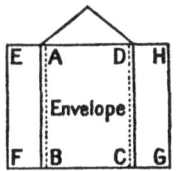 E, F, G, H is a sheet of cartridge the flaps are bent, at the dotted line so that the house stands upright when required. These paper houses are practical for play purposes, and can be packed away into a small space.	*Measuring for Drawing.* (a) For the youngest children a piece of paper, the height and width of the building, may be given. In this space the house or shop is fitted by drawing gables, windows, and doors. (b) 6–7 years. A strip of cardboard to be used as a measuring unit may be taken as the height of a storey. The children may make their buildings 1, 2, or 3 storeys high, as they choose. Windows and doors may be made with templates or by measurement. Buildings must be numbered, this is either in consecutive order of numbers, or Odd and Even may be dealt with on the two sides of the road.
(b) Pavements. (i) Paving stones.	Cartridge paper.	*Measurement.* Cut from templates Fitting these into space allowed for the path gives experience in *Area*.
(ii) Kerb Stones.	Cartridge paper.	*Measurement.* The width of the kerb should be given, and the lengths cut off from a strip of cardboard used as a unit of measure, or with the foot ruler.

82 NUMBER IN THE INFANT SCHOOL

Constructive Work.	Method.	Number in Constructive Work.
(c) Vehicles in the Street.	Waste material.	Comparison of vehicles one with another. Tall vehicles, e.g. 'bus, furniture lorry can be compared with the height of buildings. Tram-lines should be laid in lengths, the children finding how many lengths are required for length of street. The width of trams must be found by comparison with tram-lines.
(d) Safety lanes.	Silver Paper.	*Squares, circles, lines.*

VII. THE POST OFFICE

The building may be improvised with tables, chairs, garden wire-netting, and anything else that suggests post office accessories may be used.

Constructive Work.	Method.	Number involved.
Stamps. (a) In sheets.	These may be prepared for the children, by piercing several sheets (the top one divided off according to measurement of postage stamps) with an unthreaded sewing machine needle. Or, the children may make their own stamps on a sheet of paper, so measured and arranged as to get a shillings-worth down and across.	*Multiplication.* The idea of " times " in sheets of stamps. 12 penny stamps in one row. 12 × 12 penny stamps in 12 rows. Eight 1½d. stamps in one row. 12 × 8 1½d. stamps in 12 rows. Six 2d. stamps in one row. Four 3d. stamps in one row. Halfpenny stamps may be made in the double sheet, i.e. 12 in the single sheet, 24 in the double sheet. 6d., 7d., 8d., 9d., 10d., 11d. and 1s. stamps for parcels should be arranged in lines of 12.

NUMBER ARISING FROM PROJECTS

Constructive Work.	Method.	Number involved.
(b) In 2s. 6d. and 5s. books.	Stamp books could be collected for these.	*Measuring* and finding out ways of arranging 2½d., 2d., 1½d., 1d., and ½d. stamps to make 2s. 6d., 5s. worth.
Telegraph Forms.	Paper cut and ruled approximately to official size. Fractions of an inch should not be noticed in the preparation of these forms.	*Measurement.*
Parcels by Letter or Parcel Post.	Goods of any description packed in boxes, or bundles.	*Weight.*
Postal Orders.	Paper, cut, ruled, and stamped to official size.	*Measurement* in the making. Addition in the selling, poundage having to be reckoned with.

VIII. DEVELOPMENT OF AN ESTATE LEADING TO BANK

Constructive Work.	Method.	Number involved.
Houses. (a) Brickwork.	Soap boxes or cartons covered with cartridge paper.	(a) By drawing round templates the whole and half brick made in suitable proportions in relation to a real brick. These are used on sheets of cartridge paper cut to the size of the walls of the house, and give measuring experiences suitable for 6-year olds. (b) For older children, use of foot ruler with inch, ½, or ¼ inch.

Constructive Work.	Method.	Number involved.
(b) Doors and Windows.	Cartridge Paper.	*Measurement,* either by templates or the foot ruler as above.
Gardens.	An area of cardboard, or stiff cartridge paper, is allowed for each house.	This piece of land is given to the children, so that everything for the garden may be related.
(a) Paths and beds, and grass.	Rectangular, triangular, oval, and circular shapes coloured according to what they are supposed to represent.	*Shapes,* naming and arranging. *Fitting means to an end,* e.g. 1½ rectangular strips may make a path.
(b) Fencing.	Base of plasticine with match sticks stuck in.	*Measuring,* may be either with a small cardboard strip or with the foot ruler.

(For Furniture, see Furniture Shops.)

House and Estate Agents for Sale and Purchase of Houses.

(a) Sale Boards for advertisement.	Cartridge paper for boards. Skewers for poles.	*Measuring.*
(b) Money	Treasury and bank notes, value £5, £10, £20, £50, £100. Amounts should be banked for safety.	*Notation,* counting in fives, tens, twenties, fifties, hundreds.
The Bank.	Improvised from table tops, garden wire, boxes for tills.	
(a) Pass Books.	Small rectangular books.	*Measuring* in making
(b) Ledgers.	Long rectangular books. Columns for amounts.	the books and in ruling columns for cash. *Addition and Subtraction* of money.
(c) Cheques.	Plain exercise paper cut to the size of cheques.	*Measuring. Ruling lines.*

IX. Dramatic Properties

Fashioning garlands for May Day or other festivals; belts for pirates or other characters; costumes for plays

NUMBER ARISING FROM PROJECTS 85

and pageants, by the use of tape or string measures, will lead up to the use of the yard, ½, ¼, ¾ yd. measures.

Constructive Work.	Method.	Number involved in Constructive Work.
Costumes.	(i) Apron from wall paper or crinkled paper with a waistband to go round the waist.	Yard Measure, ½, ¼, ¾ yard.

| | (ii) Tunics of crinkled paper will serve for plays or Robin Hood. The Pied Piper, etc. | Measurement with yard. |

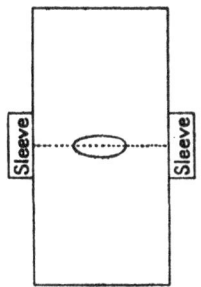

These then are some of the possible projects for the Elementary School, and they have all been worked out to show that Number may be motivated through the experiences.

Systematic schemes of Number following such experiences, will be found in subsequent chapters.

Chapter IV

NUMBER AS A SUBJECT

> "Experience suggests that most children will, before the age of eight, have acquired at least the power to work straightforward sums in the fundamental processes and in money."—*Infant and Nursery Schools Report*, p. 136.

These words practically summarize the experts' opinions on the teaching of arithmetic in the infant school. The introductory paragraph to the section on Arithmetic suggests the method for covering the scheme, the guide being the "child's natural approach", thought out in "terms of activity and experience" through his love of handling and fitting things together, through construction, "through play in which he imitates grown-up activities", and "through number games. Through these activities he becomes interested in counting, measuring, and calculating." (*Infant and Nursery Schools Report*, p. 136.)

Our first chapters have dealt with those interests of the little child which give him experience in number. Haphazard, and consequently suited to the "seemingly unordered" ways of the Nursery School child, these interests and experiences are in essence educational, but are they sufficient for the needs of the Infant School, at the stage when order and some sequence begin to be required? To-day, the child may be

NUMBER AS A SUBJECT 87

playing shops, fully occupied with the problems of " so much " and " so many " ; to-morrow, the construction of more goods being demanded, may engage all his interest in measurement ; now he is concerned with " times " or sharing operations, and again a return to counting or figure-writing is necessary. So that Number, as it only arises from the pursuit of various interests becomes a series of fragmentary experiences revealing gaps and loose ends, difficult to fill in and connect in later stages. In the ensuing chaos, it may well be that the children will be more confused than those who have followed a logical scheme of arithmetic treated as a subject and divorced from interests. The Infant School teacher has to solve the problem of the reconciliation of arithmetic as a subject, with a due consideration of the interests of the child, and at this point the aid of the mathematician-educationist is invaluable.

In the *Teaching of Arithmetic*, by Dr. David Eugene Smith, this is treated in a most enlightening manner from the two-fold standpoint of the child and the mathematician. The child's tastes and needs are made the standard, and from a consideration of these, Dr. Smith shows that the child is mentally capable of studying the subject of arithmetic at the age of 6; and as he points out, the incidental teaching so often advocated does not fully satisfy these tastes and needs, arithmetic as a subject cannot be omitted from the curriculum but must have a definite time allotted to it. He further shows that children, actively engaged in play and work all day, need more knowledge of arithmetic, because they are handling "a variety of materials and fitting them to a variety of ends".

To ensure the systematic and serious teaching of arithmetic it must be taught as a subject. Scientific investigations have proved that pupils, whose chief training has been almost exclusively in concrete problems, are not so well prepared as those who have had a fairly balanced training on concrete and abstract lines.

Simultaneously, with the working-out and development of interests, a systematic scheme of number should be developed; but the processes to be taught must originate from interests, for thus only will the principle of motive be borne in mind and treated as " the empirical situation " which is " the initiating phase in thought ".[1] No process should ever be dealt with as an abstract process, until it has been motivated and the children have come to feel that they need it, and that it is worth learning for the added power it will give them to achieve their purposes. For processes to be understood, there must be a concrete situation to give meaning and reality, leading to a true understanding.

As an illustration of such a scheme, the accompanying chart—tried and tested with children between the ages of $5\frac{1}{2}$–7 years—is given and will be worked out in future chapters. The first column deals with the interests of the children from which number experiences were evolved. Only those which could be fitted into a systematic scheme have been entered on to the chart,

[1] Dewey, *Democracy and Education*, p. 180.

NUMBER AS A SUBJECT

NUMBER CHART

I. INTERESTS.	II. NUMBER EXPERIENCES arising from I, and developed into III.	III. SYSTEMATIC SCHEME.
Interest in Games: Scoring games, e.g. hop-scotch, fish ponds, etc.	Experiences in: Counting, scoring, comparison of scores.	1. Simple Addition and Subtraction.
Projects: e.g. Shops or Multiple Stores, Transport, the Street, Zoo, Fair. Dramatic interests, Festivals, Parties, etc. (For description of projects, see Chapter III.)	Experiences with: The dozen, the shilling, the foot rule, the clock, the year.	2. Twelve, the measuring unit.
	Standard Measures: Yard, feet, inches, and fractions of the same.	3. Linear measure.
	Standard Weights: lb., ounce, and fractions of the same.	4. Avoirdupois.
	Standard Wet Measures: Pint, quart, and fractions of the same.	5. Measure of capacity.
Various life interests.	Experiences in parting and wholing.	6. Fractions.
Story and Dramatic Interests: Story and acting " How man learnt to count and use numbers ".	Experiences involving numbers over 10.	7. Notation leading to— 8. Addition and subtraction with carryings.
Projects: Development of estate leading to Estate Agents' and Bank.	Experiences with money— Pound, shillings, pence.	9. Continuation of notation. The principles and processes applied to addition and subtraction of money.
The Post Office.	Experiences in " Times ".	10. Multiplication Tables.
Shops. The Dolls' School. Factories: A Bulb Farm, etc.	Experiences in " Times ", measuring and sharing.	11. Multiplication. 12. Division.

other number experiences, not possible to dovetail into the logical scheme, were allowed to drop after they had been dealt with in passing.

Column one represents the concrete situations which gave rise to the need for number teaching. These were met in those periods devoted to projects and play ways. Column three was included on the daily programme as a definite time allotted to the teaching of number as a subject. In these periods, the children studied the number aspect and discovered with the aid of concrete material the principles underlying the various processes. Principles grasped, subsequent lessons dealt with individual difficulties of memorizing, and principles and processes were pigeon-holed in memory through practical work given in individual occupations. Concurrently, the new knowledge, acquired in the Number lessons, was used in furthering the projects or play ways which had originally given rise to the need for this knowledge.

SIMPLE ADDITION AND SUBTRACTION

I. CONCRETE SITUATIONS

The scoring games, greatly beloved of children from $5\frac{1}{2}$ years and onwards, are a natural means for giving the motive for addition and subtraction of simple numbers, and are taken as the concrete situations for leading to the more formal and abstract study of these processes. A collection of these games may be bought from any games shop, but for schoolroom use they

NUMBER AS A SUBJECT 91

must be adapted to the children's powers by simplifying both rules and number work.

Abandoning the old fixed notion of dealing with numbers 1 to 10 in the first stages of number teaching, the children should be encouraged to soar to great heights, scoring to 50, 100, or if need be beyond 100. If they want to write their scores and, not knowing how, ask for help, a direct reply is needed and at this stage is sufficient. Reasoning with regard to such numbers must not be expected, for the aim of these games is to "make the children conscious of their ignorance" of how to add numbers, or how to subtract when it comes to a comparison of scores. *Desire* will make them want *to learn* how to work the processes, and in focusing on the main work of keeping scores, we guard against dissipation of attention which would otherwise result from side-tracking to such subjects as notation. The teacher may write numbers required by the children on the blackboard or on the children's boards, rejoicing while so doing that still another bit of information has been "picked up" by the way, to be stored for later use in the study of notation.

Floor Games

1. *Hop Scotch.*

A rectangle divided into nine smaller rectangles with numbers 1 to 9 marked in them is chalked on the floor about 3 feet away from the children who sit in a semicircle with their feet to a boundary line marked with chalk.

(a) *Addition.*—Each child is provided with a small pot of beans, stones, or beads. A bean bag thrown by one of the children lands on, say 5. Each child counts and places five in a group in front of him. Another child plays on to, say 4. Each child places four beans in a group a little distance from the 5.

The teacher says, " Let us put the 5 and the 4 together, and count how many M. and J. have together." The children count and find the total is 9. An advance on this is more difficult to organize, and should not be attempted unless the teacher is capable of keeping the children occupied and seeing that they really do " play the game ". Bean bags are given to six or more children, who each have two throws and then run to their desks on which the scoring material is in readiness. From this, each child takes her own amounts, e.g. six, nine, places them in separate groups, counts the total, which is shown to the teacher who comes to verify scores.

(b) *Subtraction.*—Comparison of scores will lead to an understanding of subtraction, as worked by the process of complementary addition.

M. has 9,

J. has 5.

J. wants 6, 7, 8, 9 (placing one more bean as the figures are named) to equal M.'s score. That is, J. wants 4 more to make his score the same as M.'s. M. would have to give J. 4 more, if J. were to have 9.

NUMBER AS A SUBJECT

More Floor Games

2. *Number Arch.*

From as long a piece of cardboard as possible, several archways are cut. This framework is supported at intervals at the back, by stands of some kind, e.g. boxes, wooden bricks, etc. Over each archway a number is painted. The children are provided with ping-pong or other small, soft balls which are rolled from a distance. The score is taken from the arch under which the ball enters.

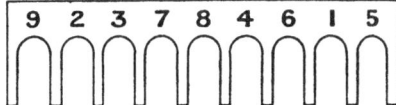

3. *Fish Ponds.*

A realistic fish pond can be made by covering the four sides of a soap, hat, or other fairly large box, with scenes depicting the wonders of the ocean. Fish of different sizes are cut in cardboard, a number is printed on each fish, and a split brass curtain ring is inserted through the mouth. The children fish with a rod of bamboo stick and string, to the end of which is attached a magnet. The score is found by the numbers on the fish.

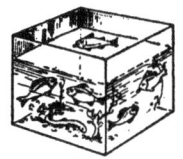 

94 NUMBER IN THE INFANT SCHOOL

4. *Skittles.*

These can be made with several empty cotton-reels stuck together, a number being painted on one. The children try to knock down the skittles with a ball thrown from a distance.

5. *Spinning Tops.*

From a circle of cardboard, an octagonal figure is cut, and divided up into triangles. Each triangle is coloured in some bright shade and numbered. The centre is pierced and the figure kept in position on a wooden meat skewer by a button-mould stuck to the under, unmarked side of the cardboard. The top is spun, and the score taken from the number where the top stops.

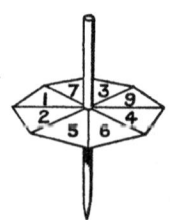

Games for Tables or Desks

1. Spinning Disc.

A circle of cardboard is prepared as above and mounted on a meat skewer which is fixed through an empty cotton reel. The base of the cotton reel is seccotined to a square platform of cardboard, at one corner of which is painted an arrow. The score is taken from the number at which the arrow points when the top ceases spinning.

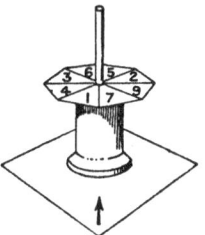

2. Dog and Bone.

A board 10 by 7 inches (a convenient size for the dual desks of the Elementary School) is prepared according to the illustration. The dog (a 1*d*. toy, or a cut-out mounted on cardboard from an illustrated paper) gets his bone by following the path and moving so many places according to the numbers turned up by a dice thrown from a dice box.

3. *Diddle-me-dot.*

A circle of paper, numbered in its divided segments is used for this game. The child closes his eyes, and with his hand held a few inches above the circle, moves it in a clockwise direction while repeating the magic words, " Diddle-me-dot." The first finger is brought down on to one of the numbers at the last syllable, and this gives a number to be scored.

4. *Racing Games.*

E.g. Snakes and Ladders, the Big Trail, etc., can be added to the collection by the enthusiastic teacher who realizes the need for variety in the children's experiences.

II. CONCRETE MATERIAL

As soon as the teacher finds interest flagging, and she feels that the time is ripe for turning the children's attention to the abstract side of the work, a halt should be called. Taking the children into her confidence, she should let them into the profound secret that all this time they have really being doing sums ! Such news is usually met with a joyful response, and games are willingly abandoned so that " sums " may be learnt in the following stages with the aid of concrete material :—

(a) *Addition*

(i) *Grouping Numbers.* The children take so many beans (number chosen by themselves or by the teacher), and make them into number pictures on their boards, and write the total by the side—

(ii) *Number groups Translated into Symbols.* The groups are formed and the total written as above. Then a group at a time is removed and replaced by the number symbol, e.g.—

Care must be taken to separate the groups.

(iii) *Use of +.* The + sign is inserted, the teacher reading the equation slowly as she writes it on the blackboard, emphasizing the *and*, e.g. 4 + 5 = 9. " Four *and* five equal nine."

Finally, she tells the children that the *and* has another and more important name, " plus."

(iv) *Finding out in how many different ways numbers can be arranged and written.* The children take 3, 4, 5, 6, etc., beans from their jars, make their own number patterns, or groups, and on different strips of paper write the equations—

$\boxed{4+2=6}$ $\boxed{1+5=6}$ $\boxed{2+4=6}$ etc.

(v) *Classifying the Analyses.* By rearranging these strips on the desk in order, the children arrive at an orderly arrangement which can be entered on one large card—

5 + 1 = 6	5 + 1 = 6
4 + 2 = 6	4 + 2 = 6
3 + 3 = 6	3 + 3 = 6
2 + 4 = 6	2 + 4 = 6
1 + 5 = 6	1 + 5 = 6

(b) *Subtraction*

It is now generally conceded that the complementary method of teaching subtraction is the better for subsequent work in mathematics, as it is claimed that it makes for greater speed and accuracy, and mathematicians urge that the method be used from the infants' school onwards. The infant teacher has not, however, been so ready to adopt this method, for taking her standpoint with the child, she has maintained that the idea behind complementary addition is abstract, and makes for a mechanical acceptance of rules rather than for reasoning and discovery on the part of the child. The idea of "taking away", on the other hand is embodied in the child's experiences, and for this reason subtraction by the method of decomposition is the child's method.

To-day, with the more advanced view of linking interests with subject-matter, difficulties of approach to methods are also disappearing, and experiments prove that it is possible to combine and thus reconcile these two methods of teaching subtraction, so that the

NUMBER AS A SUBJECT 99

first idea of decomposition leads on to the better and more approved method of complementary addition.

In the shopping activities, customers and shopkeepers are trained by the alert teacher to use both methods—the customer offers 1s. for a 7d. purchase. Sevenpence is taken away from the shilling obviously; but the shopkeeper in returning the change builds up the 1s. as he counts on from the 7d. deducted up to the 1s.

Now that the time has come for systematic work, and the motive for going more deeply into methods of subtraction has been supplied in scoring games, the children are told that they are going to learn another kind of " sum ", and concrete material is used to enable the children to discover for themselves the basic principles of the process. It is as well to let the children work in pairs, the child on the left-hand side being provided with red counters, and the child on the right-hand side being provided with blue counters.

(i) M. takes out 9 counters,

J. takes out 6 ,,

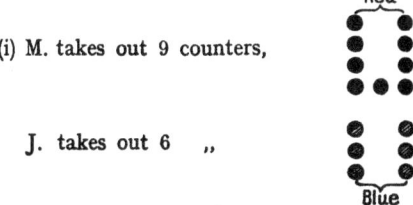

How many will M. have to give J. so that he has 9, while she has only 6 ?

100 NUMBER IN THE INFANT SCHOOL

M. counts 7, 8, 9 as she gives J. 1, 2, 3, of her red counters.

A summary is then made :—

M. had 9, she took away 3, she has 6 left. 9 take away 6 = 3.
J. wanted 9, he only had 6, M. gave him 3. 6 and 3 = 9.

Many of such examples must be worked until the teacher is sure that the children have grasped the idea, after which they pass on to :—

(ii) *The Written Statement*.

The example is worked as above, and summarized on the blackboard, the teacher repeating with emphasis the figures as they are said, and filling in the signs in place of the superfluous words, e.g.—

Decomposition.
Verbal Statement—M. has 10, she takes away 4, she has 6 left.
Written Statement—   10   —   4   =   6

Complementary.
Verbal Statement—
  J. has 6 ; J. wants 7, 8, 9, 10, i.e. 4 more to make 10.
Written Statements—
  6   +   ?   =   10.
  6   +   4   =   10.

III. INDIVIDUAL OCCUPATIONS

The knowledge can be said to be in the children's possession for it has been discovered by them. But now they have to secure this possession ; and, to insure against loss, an appeal must be made to memory. The new knowledge can be consolidated and clinched by using it once more in resorting to the scoring

NUMBER AS A SUBJECT

games; or by practice work with the following individual occupations, it may be driven home. Hand and eye work with brain in finding, sorting, and arranging the cards, and the further exercise of writing will increase understanding, and lead to greater speed, and joy in a growing sense of power over the numbers.

1. Number pictures and symbols to be placed on cards :—

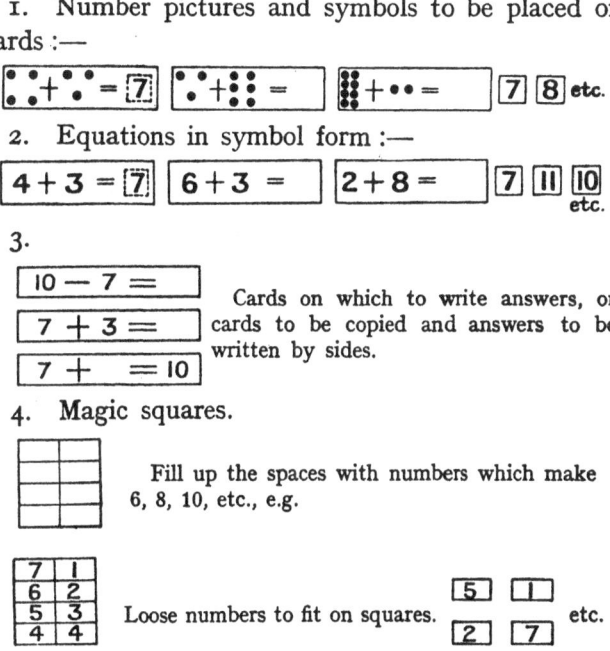

2. Equations in symbol form :—

3.

Cards on which to write answers, or cards to be copied and answers to be written by sides.

4. Magic squares.

Fill up the spaces with numbers which make 6, 8, 10, etc., e.g.

Loose numbers to fit on squares. etc.

5. *Jig-Saw Puzzles.*—A picture is cut up into shapes, and a background made on to which the shapes are transferred.

On each cut shape, a sum is written; the sum is

NUMBER IN THE INFANT SCHOOL

worked with counters, etc. Its corresponding shape will be found on the background if the sum is correct.

6. A pack of cards bearing Number symbols is given to each child. Two cards are placed in the pool by two children. Whoever gives the sum (or difference) between the two numbers first, gets the pair.

| 8 | | 2 | The child who calls 10 first, wins the cards.

7. Lotto.

| 5+1= |
| 6+2= |
| 8+1= |
| 5+4= |
| etc. |

4		8	
	9		2
7		6	
	5		1
3		10	

10		8	
	7		5
6		9	
	4		11
3		12	

| 10-2= |
| 9-3= |
| 2-1= |

8. Strips of cardboard, divided into squares of alternate colours. The strips are to be arranged end to end in as many ways as possible to make numbers, e.g. 6, 8, 10.

The sum of the strips is found from cards which are placed under the arrangements.

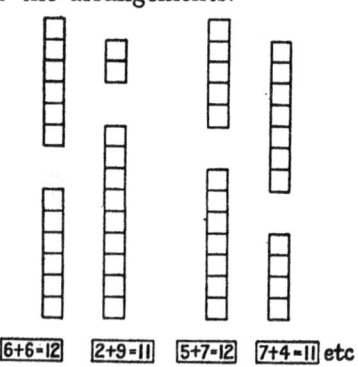

6+6=12   2+9=11   5+7=12   7+4=11 etc

CHAPTER V
THE MEASURING UNIT 12
" From the simple to the complex,
From the concrete to the abstract."

Listen to these slogans of the Infant School teacher of the past as she set about her task of drawing up elaborate Number schemes! Logical and systematic, but anæmic and lifeless, were these schemes, for they had no organic connection with the interests of the child, nor did they derive their origin from its experiences. And this was in accord with one of the aims of the school that children should put away childish things.

Number, thus prepared and presented to the 5-year-olds, was strong meat indeed. Each number up to 10 was studied intensively; all that could be known of 2 had to be discovered and learned before 3 could be attacked, similarly 3 was analysed before passing on to 4, and so on. Ten reached at last! and now much time and effort had to be expended in analysing and memorizing the parts :—

$9 + 1 = 10$; $1 + 9 = 10$; $10 - 1 = 9$; $10 - 9 = 1$; etc.

Perhaps it was as well that the information was poured into the more or less receptive minds of these babes, for such abstract truths, suitable for advanced mathematicians, could not otherwise have been ingested by these fledglings of a season's growth.

Months and years dragged on before the numbers 10 to 20 had been treated in like manner, after which the 10's table was built up, and then memory was taxed further with regard to notation. Confusion reigned in baby minds, and from the dark disordered soil, only too often sprang boredom and hatred of all Number work. At the outset difficulties were anticipated, and even created, for the children; knowledge which could, and should have been picked up along with experience, and used as a background for the study of principles, was crammed by forced methods into the children's minds.

A logical scheme, divorced from purposeful play experiences, setting out with an analysis of simple numbers followed by the facts and principles of notation, is exceedingly difficult for little children. It demands processes of abstract thought which are quite beyond their range. A more profitable way of building on the experiences described in the previous chapters, and one which follows psychological principles and balances the two phases of Number teaching, is to take 12 as the next unit of measure. The children, in working out various projects and play activities, meet with it in one or more situations.

As in life they have found :—

    A. The dozen is measured by   12 articles.
    B. The shilling is measured by   12 pennies.
    C. The foot ruler is measured by   12 inches.
    D. The day is measured by   12 hours.
    E. The year is measured by   12 months.

THE MEASURING UNIT 12

A consideration of these five quantities as measured by the 12, will give further reasons for following up the experiences gained through them by definite and systematic Number schemes.

(i) Approached through the concrete experiences of playways or projects, a need for a study of the measuring unit is created, and arithmetic, as a subject, continues to have its part in the course.

(ii) As the various quantities measured by 12 are encountered in different concrete situations and studied through concrete materials, comparisons of one quantity with another will be made. For example the shilling as measured by the 12 pennies can be compared with the foot rule, measured by the 12 inches. Thus the children's reasoning powers will be kept up to the maximum, as they are helped to see the relations existing between the different quantities.

(iii) Much incidental knowledge will be gained as the children work, enlightenment will come almost imperceptibly both in the counting and writing of numbers over 12, and all the time a more secure foundation for ideas of notation will be in the making.

In many Infant Schools, we have developed Number schemes from experiences in which the children have met with 12. The following examples of such schemes taken from Students' note-books may be suggested to teachers who are attempting to make Arithmetic a living reality to their children.

A. THE DOZEN AS MEASURED BY THE 12 ARTICLES
I. CONCRETE SITUATIONS

Constructive work in making goods for shops is the best method of dealing with the dozen. The children should be encouraged to find for themselves goods sold by the dozen, either by being taken in school hours for excursions to the shops, or by asking for information at home.

(a) *The Greengrocer.*

Bananas or oranges. Made in clay, or by drawing and cutting out shapes on postcards.

(b) *The Grocer.*

Soap tablets in clay. Match-boxes, Oxo cubes, etc. Dummy packets in stiff paper.

(c) *The Draper.*

Button cards. These can be drawn on stiff paper, or real buttons can be attached to cards.

(d) *The Stationer.*

Pencils and rubbers borrowed from the stationery cupboard can be made up into dozens; or old pencil ends may be hoarded for the purpose, and india rubbers cut into small pieces.

Small exercise books for the dolls made from sheets of paper, and tied together in dozens.

(e) *The Dairy.*

Eggs made in clay.

(f) *The Confectioner.*

Fancy cakes, sausage rolls, etc., modelled from a flour and salt mixture. $\frac{3}{4}$ lb. of flour to $\frac{1}{4}$ lb. of kitchen salt mixed with sufficient water to make a stiff dough gives cheap, clean, and realistic results.

II. CONCRETE MATERIAL AND III. INDIVIDUAL OCCUPATIONS

The goods themselves will be used for concrete materials and for individual occupations. By arranging

THE MEASURING UNIT 12

them in different ways, the children will be enabled to see :—

½ dozen = 6 ;	the dozen could be arranged as 6 + 6
¼ dozen = 3 ;	,, ,, 3 + 3 + 3 + 3
½ dozen + ¼ dozen = 6 + 3 ;	,, ,, ,, 6 + 3 + 3
½ dozen + ¼ dozen = ¾ dozen ;	,, ,, ,, 9 + 3

Or, with single goods, the dozen can be made up in the following ways :—

$$11 + 1 = 12$$
$$10 + 2 = 12$$
$$9 + 3 = 12, \text{ etc.}$$

Or, in twos :—
  2 + 2 + 2 + 2 + 2 + 2 = 12
Or, in threes :—
  3 + 3 + 3 + 3
Or, in fours :—
  4 + 4 + 4
Or, in sixes :—
  6 + 6

N.B.—Grouping and getting the idea of " times " for multiplication.

B. THE SHILLING AS MEASURED BY THE 12 PENNIES

I. CONCRETE SITUATIONS

Stage 1.—Free Shop Play.

Life experiences imitated in play activities, e.g. shopping, Christmas bazaars, railway and 'bus journeys, etc., provide opportunities for dealing with the shilling.

The teacher, while actively participating in the play, must be on the alert and help to regulate the experiences, in order that she may recognize and seize the opportune moment for definite teaching. As long as the attitude of the children is one of serious absorption, play will be of value; but if there are signs of waning interest, shown either in play flagging or degenerating into fooling, the teacher must take warning and realize that the play is ceasing to afford adequate stimulation : " With increasing maturity, activity which does not give back results of tangible and visible achievement loses its interest. Play then changes to fooling and, if habitually indulged in, is demoralizing. Observable results are necessary to enable persons to get a sense and a measure of their own powers." (*Democracy and Education*, p. 239.)

If their energies are dissipated in fooling, the children require more knowledge before they can continue their play; the shops must be closed, and the aim of finding out how to shop quickly and accurately must be brought before the children's consciousness definitely and clearly.

Stage 2.—Directed Shopping.

Aim of Lesson—to find out the different ways in which a shilling can be spent.

Apparatus.—(i) Envelopes for each child containing 12 oranges at 1*d*. each; 6 bananas at 2*d*. each; 4 pears at 3*d* each; 3 grape fruits at 4*d*. each; 2 bunches of grapes at 6*d*. each.

12 cardboard pennies for each child.

(ii) Large shop front on blackboard, with fruits, and prices to correspond with those in children's envelopes.

THE MEASURING UNIT 12

Problems and Method.

1. *Finding the number of 1d. goods that can be bought for 1s.*—A make-believe order is given. A shillingsworth of oranges is ordered from the shop, these are to be " sent home ".

The teacher removes 12 oranges from the shop, while the children take out the oranges from their envelopes, place 1d. on each until all their pence are used, when they find they have bought 12 oranges for 1s.

2. *Number of 2d. goods that can be bought for 1s.*—Bananas at 2d. each are dealt with in the same way.

Pay *one* twopence, *two* twopences, *three* twopences, etc., up to *six* twopences, and thus make up 1s.

3. *Number of 3d., 4d., and 6d. goods that can be bought for 1s.*—As in 2.

After the children have had experience of this more formal type they should revert to their free shopping experiences. If the balance is maintained between these two types—free and formal—attention may soon be directed to a study of the possibilities of the money apart from the shopping, and as the children deal with the concrete material, work of a more abstract nature can be introduced.

II. CONCRETE MATERIAL

Apparatus.—12 cardboard pennies for each child.

Children's Purpose.—To find out in how many different ways they can group 12 pence.

Teacher's Purpose.—The Analysis of a Shilling.

110 NUMBER IN THE INFANT SCHOOL

Problems and Method.

1. *Finding the different ways in which* 1s. *worth of pennies can be grouped.*—The following arrangements may be made by the children :—

(i) 12 pennies in a straight line of ones.

(ii) Pennies arranged in twos ; then in threes ; fours ; sixes. After the groups have been made, the children should gather them in their hands, and make statements :—

    (a) 12 pennies   = 1s.
    (b) One twopence
        Two twopences
        Three ,,   etc.
        Six   ,,   = 1s.
    (c) One threepence
        Two threepences
        Three ,,
        Four   ,,   = 1s.
    (d) Repeat with fourpences and sixpences.

2. *Other ways of arranging the* 12 *pennies.*—The children should then find other ways of arranging the shillingsworth of pennies, e.g.

(i) Beginning with the 12 pennies in a line, move 1*d.* over to the right-hand side of the desk, then they have 11*d.* + 1*d.* = 1*s.*

(ii) Moving 1*d.* at a time from left to right, children arrive at the analysis of the 12 pennies :—

$$\begin{array}{cc} d. & d. \end{array}$$
$$11 + 1 = 1s.$$
$$10 + 2 = 1s.$$
$$9 + 3 = 1s.$$
$$8 + 4 = 1s.$$
$$7 + 5 = 1s.$$
$$6 + 6 = 1s.$$

This newly acquired knowledge is used in further shop plays, and the teacher must now be on the watch for the next stage when she deems the time has come for dealing with problems of change.

I. CONCRETE SITUATIONS

Stage 1.—Free Shop Play.

With a silver shilling in place of the 12 pennies, the children should set out again on shopping expeditions. Difficulties in getting and giving the right change necessitate the closing of the shop in order that the children may learn to deal with the process of subtraction of money.

Stage 2.—Directed Shopping.

Aim of Lesson.—Giving change.

Apparatus.—(i) Large shop front mounted on blackboard with 12 toys arranged in couples and marked. 11*d.*, 1*d.* ; 10*d.*, 2*d.* ; 9*d.*, 3*d.* ; 8*d.*, 4*d.* ; 7*d.*, 5*d.* ; 6*d.*, 6*d.*

(ii) For the children who work in pairs of shopkeepers and customers.

Shopkeepers.—12 cut-out toys corresponding to those on the blackboard, and 12 pennies.

Customers.—1 silver shilling.

First Purchase.—One child comes to the shop front and buys, say, a golliwog at 4*d.*

Steps in giving change.
  (i) She gives the shopkeeper 1s.
  (ii) Shopkeeper gives the customer 12*d.*

(iii) Customer gives shopkeeper 4d., then receives toy and finds that she has 8d. change.

Second Purchase.—The teacher chooses the second toy, valued at 8d. (This is advisable so that she can balance the shilling which has been broken, and thus lead to a clearer idea of complementary addition.) 8d. is given to the shopkeeper who then makes a whole shilling with the odd 4d. acquired in the last transaction.

Children then change places. The shopkeepers become customers and vice versa.

Several transactions can be accomplished as above, then an advance may be made by dealing with giving change in the following way :—

(i) Customer gives shopkeeper 1s.

(ii) Shopkeeper changes the customer's 1s. into pence and takes amount of purchase from it, say 5d.

(iii) Shopkeeper gives customer 5d. toy and 7d. change.

As in the earlier experiences, the free and more directed forms of play go hand in hand and lead to a need for more abstract knowledge, so this development in knowledge and power will lead to further needs, and now the children can concentrate on the concrete material of the money apart from the concrete situation of shopping.

II. CONCRETE MATERIAL

Children's Purpose.—To find out the different ways of giving change from 1s.

Teacher's Purpose.—The " parting and wholing " of the shilling so that the method of subtraction by decomposition may gradually give place to complementary addition.

Apparatus.—One shilling and 12 cardboard pennies for each child.

Steps in giving Change.

(i) The shilling is changed into its equivalent in pence.

(ii) Decomposition.—" Parting " the shilling.—So many pennies are taken away from the whole group of 12 pence, e.g., $12d. - 9d. = 3d.$

(iii) Complementary addition.—" Wholing " the shilling again, $3d. + 9d. = 12d.$

(iv) Arriving at the conclusion—
$$12d. - 9d. = 3d.$$
$$9d. + ? = 12d.$$

III. INDIVIDUAL OCCUPATIONS

A hectographed sheet arranged as below is given to the children who draw in the right number of fruits to balance the shilling, write the prices under each, and count up the number of pennies, twopences, threepences, etc.

114 NUMBER IN THE INFANT SCHOOL

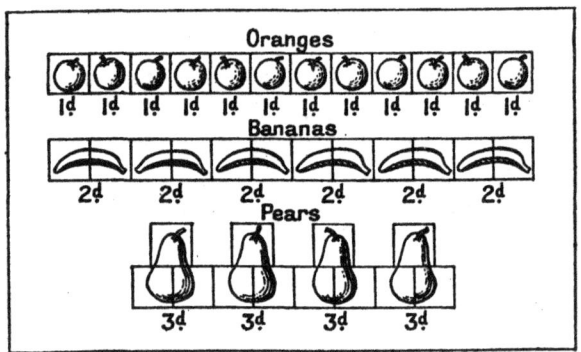

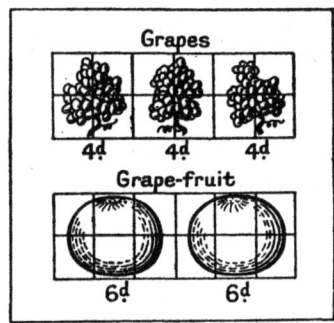

Number Cards.

"*Penny and Shilling pictures.*"

(i)

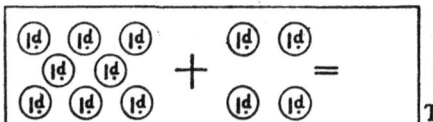 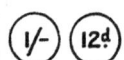

The two sides of the shilling. On one side, 1*s*. is marked, and 12*d*. on the other.

THE MEASURING UNIT 12

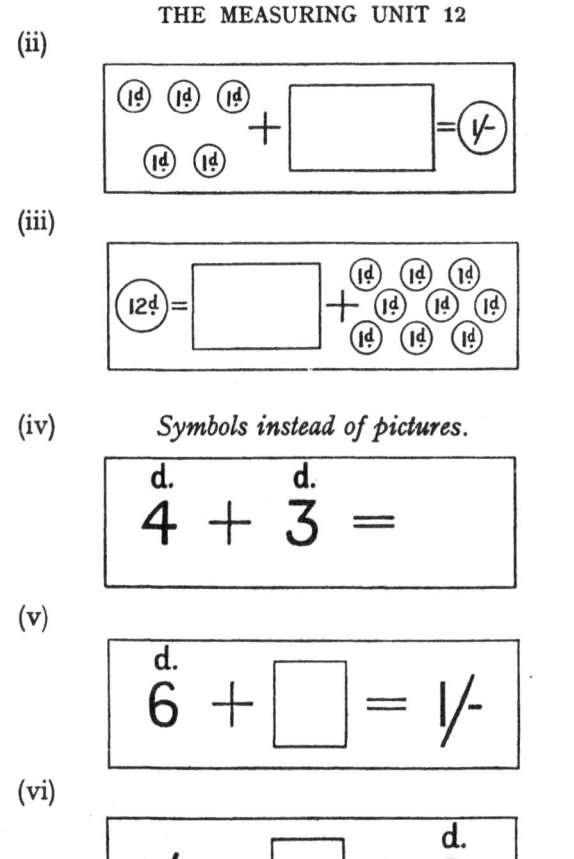

Following on from the practice work of the Individual Occupations, another class lesson may be taken when the teacher encourages the children to systematize their knowledge. The following table should be built up on the blackboard, and copied into books.

d.	d.	d.	d.	d.	d.
11	+ 1	= 12	12	− 1	= 11
10	+ 2	= 12	1	+ 11	= 12
9	+ 3	= 12	12	− 2	= 10
8	+ 4	= 12	2	+ 10	= 12
7	+ 5	= 12	12	− 3	= 9
6	+ 6	= 12	3	+ 9	= 12
5	+ 7	= 12	12	− 4	= 8
4	+ 8	= 12	4	+ 8	= 12
3	+ 9	= 12	12	− 5	= 7
2	+ 10	= 12	5	+ 7	= 12
1	+ 11	= 12	6	− 6	= 0
			6	+ 6	= 12

CHAPTER VI

THE MEASURING UNIT 12 (*continued*)

C. THE FOOT RULE AS MEASURED BY 12 INCHES

I. CONCRETE SITUATIONS

The following suggestions for motivating the study of measurement, having been worked out in the large classes of the Elementary School, are practicable and bring before the children their need for a knowledge of linear measurement with the foot rule as a standard.

1. *Projects.*

See Chapter III. Shops, e.g. Stationer's. Festivals, e.g. Christmas. Lunch or Party Equipment. The Zoo. Development of an Estate.

2. *Play Interests.*

(i) *Jumping.*—A game for the hall or playground. The children are divided into teams, take distances and stand in lines, with the leader of each team holding a piece of chalk in her hand while her feet toe a chalk line marked on the floor. At a given signal from the teacher, the first child in each team jumps as far as possible, marks with chalk her landing-place, and writes her name. When all the team have jumped and recorded in the same way, a comparison of the leaps concludes the game, and as the children recognize the difficulty of giving exact statements as to "how much longer or shorter," they should be led to the need of a standard measure.

(ii) *The Desert Island Game.*—This is played by marking out as large a rectangle as possible on the schoolroom floor to represent the desert island on which the shipwrecked class is cast. While waiting for a passing ship to rescue them, the captain (the teacher) suggests measuring the island so that an idea of its size may be given to their friends on their return home. As the only available measure, the foot, is suggested, several children step the diameter of the island, and the results, written in the captain's pocket-book are as follows :—

Captain, 32 feet. Lucy 41 feet. Elsie 47 feet.
Jack 45 ,, Tommy, 38 ,, Bobby, 43 ,,

As soon as a ship is sighted (i.e. when the teacher sees that interest in the measuring is flagging) the castaways are taken off and shipped back to England. Here the need for standard rulers is found out. For in the course of "telling their experiences", they cannot reconcile the differences and discrepancies in the number of feet and the size of shoes.

(iii) *The Game of Allotments.*—Each member of the class (teacher included) is to have an allotment of the same size, say 20 feet by 15 feet. The teacher, as the tallest, measures out her parcel of ground with her feet, after which the smallest child is chosen to measure his piece of land, and then the other children follow.

THE MEASURING UNIT 12   119

It will not be long before the "unfairness" of the arrangement makes itself evident to the children, and a demand for a uniform measure be made.

(iv) *Comparison of Children's heights.*—(*a*) The children are required to line up in order of height as for drill—the tallest at the front and the shortest at the end. From the ensuing confusion, as comparisons are made, emerges the suggestion that the matter could be settled by standing back to back. When the line is arranged, it is proposed to obtain a permanent record and the next step is to measure against the wall.

(*b*) Sheets of kitchen paper, or lengths of wall paper, are pinned to the wall, and the children in groups of eight or ten stand with their backs to the wall. The teacher goes along the line, placing a book on each head in turn, and as she does this the child draws a line along the underside of the book and turns to write its name on the line.

(*c*) Comparisons of heights follow :—Doris is taller than Jenny, the smallest girl in the class is Lottie, etc., and it is soon seen that a more accurate and concise method must be found.

II. CONCRETE MATERIAL

The construction of the foot ruler leads to the second stage in the work. Each child is given an unmarked strip of stiff cartridge paper, 1 foot long by 1 inch wide. They are told that this measure is called 1 foot, and they print 1 foot on one side of the ruler.

They are then invited to use these rulers for measuring heights on the wall, allotments, or in any concrete situation where the need for a ruler has arisen. And now the reiteration of " so many feet and so much more " will bring home the need for a smaller measure. An examination of a " big " boy's or girl's ruler will make this point still clearer. If any child is acquainted already with the name inch, she will be asked to tell the others, if not the teacher will give this information. A new problem now confronts them, how to discover the number of inches in one foot, and this can be solved by one of the following methods :—

(*a*) A packet of 14 or more paper strips, 1 inch square, is given to the children to fit on to the ruler, and they make the discovery that there are 12 inches in 1 foot. After pasting these on to the ruler they number the divisions 1 inch to 12 inches.

(*b*) Older children might be given a 2-inch unit of measurement, on which they should write 2 inches after they have been told its length. The problem is to find how many times the 2 inch goes into the foot ruler, and is solved by measuring the 2-inch strip six times along the ruler. They then count the 2-inch spaces and discover that there are 12 inches in 1 foot.

Again using the marked ruler in connection with the concrete situation, the children find that they can measure anything which is a multiple of 2 inch, but a further difficulty arises for they have no means of representing the odd inches 1, 3, 5, 7, 9 and 11 inches.

THE MEASURING UNIT 12 (*cont.*) 121

The solution of the problem may present itself to the children in two steps :—

(i) Making a line down the middle of each division—but how find the middle ? This will lead to

(ii) Folding the 2-inch strip in half, and so obtaining two single inches.

The inches are then transferred to the foot ruler, and the discoveries made by the children summarized :—

12 inches = 1 foot.
6 (2 inches) = 1 foot.

A return to the concrete situation in which the need for the ruler originated, enables the children to complete that experience by measuring in feet and inches, after which, interest in measurement may be further stimulated by a discussion on,

Workers who Use the Foot Ruler.

School teachers and children.—Measuring for handwork, measuring heights, margins, etc.

Builders and Architects.—Measuring rooms, houses, school buildings and playing fields, ceilings, walls, etc.

Carpenters.—Making furniture, e.g. tables, chairs, desks, etc.

Another constructive experience, involving a repetition of the former experience in another form, may be the

Making of a Folding Ruler.

Give each child four 4-inch strips of stiff cartridge paper.

Problem 1.—With foot rulers already constructed, find how many 4-inch strips will be required to make the folding ruler. The children find that three 4-inch strips are required, and hinge the strips with binding tape or paper.

Problem 2.—Marking the single inches. The children should be required to find out how to divide their remaining 4-inch strip into single inches. Folding the 4-inch strip in half, and then in quarters gives 4 single inches which are transferred to the folding foot rule, now ready for use in school, and at home to measure anything that attracts the children's interest.

III. INDIVIDUAL OCCUPATIONS

(i) A packet of paper strips, of lengths varying from 1 inch to 11 inches is given to each child. The children take out two strips at a time, measure and write the length on each strip, join the strips by placing end to end, find the total length, and make a " sum " to show the result :—

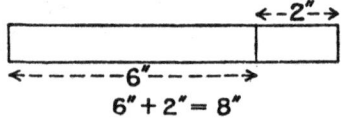

N.B.—The importance of proving these sums cannot be too strongly urged. The children must not be allowed to write the sum from memory without testing with rulers.

(ii) Each child is given a packet containing eleven unmarked foot rulers, and lengths measuring from 1 inch to 11 inch. The children measure and mark the latter, then cut off similar lengths from the foot rulers and find out the remaining lengths, thus getting

THE MEASURING UNIT 12 (cont.) 123

exercise in subtraction by decomposition. Putting the pieces together again, helps to impress and clarify the idea of subtraction by the complementary method.

(iii) Analysis of the foot ruler. The aim of this exercise is to systematize the work done hitherto.

Apparatus for each Child.—A packet containing two strips of each of the measures 1 inch to 12 inches, also the foot ruler. The children make the 12-inch ruler in as many ways as possible using two strips for each complete ruler. The foot rules are then arranged in systematic order, and the results written in tabular form:—

Inches. Inches. Foot. Inches.
11 + 1 = 1 or 12
10 + 2 = 1 or 12
9 + 3 = 1 or 12 etc.

(iv) *Connection between the shilling as measured by 12d., and the foot as measured by 12 inches.*—Sum cards are given to the children. In the talk preceding the lesson, the children notice that the sums on one side of the card deal with shillings and pence, on the other side feet and inches. The concrete material of pence and foot rulers should be used. " There is a secret in these sums. Who can find it out ? " This is a magic remark for it stimulates eager thought and intent purpose. On discovering that the answers are identical, the children are asked for the reason and it will be found that 12, as the measuring unit, is taking its place in the consciousness of the children.

s.	d.	ft.	in.
4	6	4	6
+ 2	4	+ 2	4

s.	d.	ft.	in.
3	9	3	9
+ 4	5	+ 4	5

s.	d.	ft.	in.
1	6	1	6
+	3	+	3

s.	d.	ft.	in.
5	0	5	0
+ 4	9	+ 4	9

s.	d.	ft.	in.
2	8	2	8
+ 1	7	+ 1	7

s.	d.	ft.	in.
6	5	6	5
+ 3	10	+ 3	10

"Story" Sums

1. Winnie can jump 18 inches, Dick jumps 3 inches further, how many inches does Dick jump?

2. Toby jumps 3 inches further than Mary who jumps 21 inches, how far does Toby jump?

3. Lucy can swim 27 inches and Timothy 6 inches less, how far can Timothy swim?

THE MEASURING UNIT 12 (cont.) 125

4. May can swim 18 inches further than Basil who swims 22 inches, how far can May swim?

5. The school hall is 20 feet long and if Winnie jumps 2 feet how many jumps will she take to jump from beginning to end?

6. May is 26 inches tall and Daisy is 2 ft. 5 in., how much taller is Daisy?

7. Poppy is 2 ft. 2 in. tall and Jack is 3 feet. How much taller is Jack?

8. Robin is 2 inches shorter than Leslie who is 3 feet. How tall is Robin?

Inches.	Inches.	Inches.	ft.	in.
6 +	6 =		=	
16 +	8 =		=	
10 +	5 =		=	
9 +	7 =		=	
5 +	11 =		=	
d.	d.	pence.	s.	d.
3 +	10 =		=	
5 +	9 =		=	
7 +	8 =		=	
10 +	6 =		=	
12 +	6 =		=	
9 +	11 =		=	

D. THE CLOCK MEASURED BY THE 12 HOURS

I. CONCRETE SITUATIONS

Suggestions for Motivating the Study of Time.

1. It requires very little stimulus to arouse ambition in the children to tell the time. They already know that they must be in time for school, and there are fixed times for play, lunch, and going home. All these experiences in the routine work of the day make

K

children aware that time has continually to be taken into account.

2. The motive for learning to tell the time may come from play interests such as shops, the Zoo, trains, etc. See Chapter III.

3. A clock face may be placed in a prominent position in the class-room and left for the children to examine and handle in their free periods. Before interest in the activity flags, it should be suggested to the children that they make their own clocks so that they may learn to tell the time.

II. CONCRETE MATERIAL
Constructing the Clock and Learning to tell the Time

1. *Constructing the Clock.*

A circle of paper, cut in stiff cartridge paper, is given to each child. A blue mark gives the position for the 12.

The teacher has a large clock face to correspond with the children's, also a model clock which is examined by the children, when they notice that the 12 is the highest point on the clock face. They are told that the blue mark on their circles has been made for them and gives them the starting-point. The children then place the clock face in position and print 12 below this mark. The teacher moves the hands of the model clock face in a straight line from 12 and 6.

Where will 6 be printed on the clocks? The fact

THE MEASURING UNIT 12 (*cont.*) 127

that the hands divide the teacher's clock face into two equal parts is apparent to the children and by folding the circles from the 12 they find the position of the 6. Folding the half circle again from the 6 to 12, and placing it on the model clock, the children will see 3 and 9 on the quarter circle lines, and the children will then complete this part of the constructive work. Further examination of the clock face reveals the fact that two more figures have to be printed in each quarter of the circle. In order that the children may discover the positions of these figures for themselves, a puzzle may be given them.

A quarter of a circle, corresponding in size to their quarter circles, is cut into three equal segments. With these, the children make the following discoveries :—

(*a*) The segments are equal to each other.

(*b*) The three segments fit into each quarter of the circle.

(*c*) The two spaces between the segments, when fitted into the quarter circle, give the places for the missing numbers on the clock face, 1, 2 ; 4, 5 ; 7, 8 ; 10, 11.

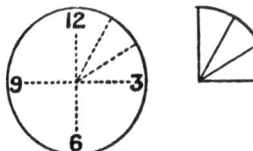

The remaining figures for the clock faces are now filled in, the hands—small and large, which are best cut by the teacher before the lesson—affixed, and now the clock is ready for use.

2. Learning to Tell the Time.

(i) *The Hours.*—To show the connection with the children's lives, the teacher tells the story of "Our Busy Day", and as they move the clock hands to mark their successive activities the children should discover that the big hand on the 12 always says "o'clock" while the little hand on the figures says "how many" o'clock.

Putting the hands in position, the teacher says,

"At 7 o'clock, we get up,"

then, slowly turning the hands round the clock, she goes on

"At 8 o'clock we have breakfast
At 9 o'clock we go to school
At 10 o'clock we have lessons
At 11 o'clock we go to play
At 12 o'clock we go home
At 1 o'clock we have dinner, etc."

N.B.—It is most important that teacher and children move the hands round the clock in the correct direction, for it must be realized by the teacher that the clockwise movement is necessary for an understanding of time.

(ii) *The Half-Hours.*—In constructing the clock the children found half the clock face by folding their papers. This fact should be recalled and linked up with the discovery of the half hours. Beginning with both hands on the 12, and then moving the big one round to the 6, the children will see that the big hand has travelled half-way round the clock when it reaches the six so that we say "half-past." Now a fresh chapter can be added to the Busy Day chronicle,

THE MEASURING UNIT 12 (*cont.*)

the children tracing on the clock face each duty and experience at its appointed time.

> At 7 o'clock we get up.
> At half-past 7 we lay the breakfast.
> At 8 o'clock we have breakfast.
> At half-past 8 we clear away the breakfast.
> At 9 o'clock we go to school, etc.

(iii) *The Quarter Hours*, i.e. quarter-past and a quarter-to, can be dealt with in the same way.

(iv) *The Minutes.*—Further observation of the clock will lead to the discovery of the little spaces between the hours. " What are these ? The big hand will soon travel from one to another of these. Let us sit still and see how many we can count while the big hand moves from one of these little spaces to the next." The teacher leads and all count to 6o. If an hour-glass is shown at the same time, a better understanding of the meaning of a minute will be gained as the sands drop through and the hand traverses the tiny space. The name " minute " should be given, and then follows the marking of the spaces in their clocks. As this is difficult, some teachers prefer to do it themselves, taking the clocks home to mark in the small divisions, for the children to use in learning to tell the time with minutes. If the children are to mark them in for themselves, the best plan is to give them paper segments subdivided into five from which they are measured off on their clock faces.

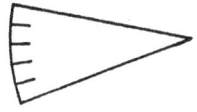

Learning to tell the time in Minutes.

This gives a golden example of the virtue of making haste slowly, for it requires much time on the children's part and consequently great patience on the part of the teacher. The children should be allowed freedom to move their clock hands as they like, at first experimenting and moving them on for long or short distances, counting as they do the number of minutes from the 12 to the place where the big hand has stopped. This interest can be maintained and directed by the teacher as she goes round the class and listens to the observations. The more intelligent children eagerly remark that they have found that there are 15 minutes between the figures 12 and 3; 25 between 12 and 5; or that the big hand has been placed 18 minutes past the 12 and so on.

The children who are not so perceptive may be helped to count the number of minutes as they change the hands about to any positions they like. Such experimental experiences will pave the way for the more serious study of the minutes. Placing the two hands on the 12, so that everyone's clock says 12 o'clock, the teacher will tell them that they are all going to find out what o'clock it says, when the little hand remains on the 12 and the big hand travels on by itself to the other figures. (The fact that the little hand is moving very slowly throughout the hour need not be dealt with at this point.)

The children very readily discover the time as

THE MEASURING UNIT 12 (*cont.*)

measured by minutes when the big hand touches the 1, 2, 3, 4, 5, 6.

     5 minutes *past* 12
    10   ,,   ,, 12
    15   ,,   ,, 12 (or a quarter *past* 12)
    20   ,,   ,, 12
    25   ,,   ,, 12
    30   ,,   ,, 12 (or half *past* 12)

A pause must be made, and the fact that the big hand is getting farther and farther away from 12 o'clock, and nearer and nearer 1 o'clock is noticed, then the children may be told that now we count the number of minutes *before* or *to* the next hour, and so we arrive at

    25 minutes *before*, or *to* 1
    20   ,,   ,, or *to* 1
    15   ,,   ,, or *to* 1 (or a quarter *to* 1)
    10   ,,   ,, or *to* 1
     5   ,,   ,, or *to* 1
    1 o'clock.

The symmetrical arrangement of the figures, and the comparison of the statements made, according to the positions of the minute hand *past* or *to* the hour afford much entertainment to the children, and help to fix the facts thus acquired firmly in the children's minds. "*The Past and To*" game may be played, two children holding their clocks up in front of the class, and in turn they give the time in minutes *past* and *to* the hour.

E.g., between 12 and 1 o'clock.

```
 5 minutes past 12
10    ,,    ,, 12
15    ,,    ,, 12 (or a quarter past 12)
 5 minutes to   1
10    ,,    ,,  1
15    ,,    ,,  1 (or a quarter to 1)
```

The Five Times Table.

Building up the five times table comes in natural sequence, even though the children may not, as yet, have had any dealings with multiplication tables.

Remembering that, at this age, counting is still an interest, the children may be asked to find how many minutes there are round the whole clock. They will probably count them out in ones, then in groups thus :—

> 1 group of 5 minutes = 5 minutes.
> 2 groups of 5 minutes = 10 minutes.
> 3 groups of 5 minutes = 15 minutes, and so forth.

Then a still shorter way of expressing this in writing will be shown to the children thus :—

$$1 \times 5 = 5$$
$$2 \times 5 = 10$$
$$3 \times 5 = 15, \text{ etc.}$$

III. INDIVIDUAL OCCUPATIONS

Cards with drawings of clocks for the children to write the time by the side ; or vice versa, with times written for the children to make the drawings :—

THE MEASURING UNIT 12 (cont.)

"Story" Sums

1. A boy went to school at 9 o'clock and left at 12 o'clock. How long was he at school?

2. Harry and Charlie went to school at 2 o'clock. Harry was sick and went home at half past 3 o'clock, but Charlie stayed till 4 o'clock. How long was each boy at school?

3. Pat's father is a night-watchman. He goes on duty at 8 o'clock for ten hours. What time can he leave in the morning?

4. If Pat's father takes an hour to get home in the morning, an hour for breakfast and then goes to bed, how many hours can he have in bed before Pat comes home at 12 o'clock from school?

5. At half-past four Josie lends her scooter to Billy for a quarter of an hour. When does he have to give it back?

6. Mary gets up at 7 and takes half an hour to wash and dress, quarter of an hour to feed her rabbits. What is the time when she has finished?

7. Jack goes to bed at half-past six. His bath takes a quarter of an hour. What time is left before his mother comes to read to him at 7?

8. The Scripture lesson began at half-past nine and went on for twenty minutes. What time was it then?

9. At half-past three, teacher says " In a quarter of an hour put your paints away." What time do the children stop painting?

10. Susie made a cake, put it in the oven at a

quarter to 11 and baked it for three-quarters of an hour. When did she take it out?

E. The Year Measured by the 12 Months

I. Concrete Situations

1. May follow on from study of time measured by the clock.

2. Calendars may be wanted for Christmas bazaars, the stationer's shop, or to take home for Christmas presents.

3. Talks on new term, new month, making of weather or nature charts.

II. Concrete Material

Hectographed sheets ruled in columns down and across for name of month, days and dates are given to the children.

Writing lessons may be used for filling in months and days, number lessons should deal with the number side of the work—filling in dates.

N.B.—Numbers beyond 12. The children are "picking up" information which can be clinched later. Explanations, or reasons for method of writing numbers, are out of place here unless children seek for them themselves.

Method of filling in dates—

(i) For the first month or two, the dates may be filled in in consecutive order. Children find New Year's Day, then write in remainder of dates.

(ii) After filling in one or two months in this way the work should be stopped, and the children required to notice the dates which fell on all the Thursdays, Fridays, Saturdays, etc., of the month. How many days between? If the first of the month

THE MEASURING UNIT 12 (*cont.*)   135

is on a Thursday, what will be the date (the following Thursday), the second Thursday, the third Thursday, the fourth Thursday of the month ?

Counting in sevens will be dealt with, after which the children should attempt to complete the calendar by using this table of sevens.

Before mounting and pinning the calendars together, the completed months should be used for making the following discoveries :—

(*a*) The year is made up of 12 months.

(*b*) Each month is made up of 4 weeks, and some odd days, excepting February which is exactly 4 weeks. (Omit any mention of Leap Year, unless it happens to be Leap Year.)

(*c*) The months are divided into four seasons ; the number of months in each can be found and written under the headings spring, summer, autumn, winter.

(*d*) The number of days in the year :—

January,	31 days.	February, 28 days.	April,	30 days.
March,	31 ,,		June,	30 ,,
May,	31 ,,		September,	30 ,,
July,	31 ,,		November,	30 ,,
August,	31 ,,			
October,	31 ,,			120 ,,
December,	31 ,,			
	217 ,,			

         217 days
          28 ,,
         120 ,,
         ───
         365 ,,

(*e*) The 12 months are divided into two equal piles, and it is found that ½ year = 6 months. The 12 months are divided into four equal piles, and it is found that ¼ year = 3 months. Taking ½ a year and ¼ year, the children discover that ¾ year = 9 months.

The children will enjoy arranging the months in

as many ways as possible. Compare dozen, shilling, foot rule, etc.

They will find that when 1 month of the year is gone, 11 months are left. 2 months of the year are gone, 10 months are left, etc.

III. INDIVIDUAL OCCUPATIONS

Sum Cards with stories to be worked with the calendars, e.g. :—

1. Mary's baby sister was born in January. When will she be 3 months, 6 months, 9 months old ?

2. Jack's baby brother is 9 months old. How many more months will there be before he is a year, or 12 months, old ?

3. January, February, March — in School.
April — Holidays.
May, June, July — School.
August — Holidays.
September, October, November — School.
December — Holidays.

How many months in school ? On holiday ?

4. Jill's birthday is on the 25th of September. How many months is that before Christmas ?

5. The first day of spring is on March 21st. Find Midsummer Day which comes three months later.

6. Daisy's birthday is on December 27th. She says it is too near Christmas, so her Mother says she shall have her birthday party six months later when she is half a year older, when will Daisy have her party ?

THE MEASURING UNIT 12 (*cont.*) 137

Now comparison of other quantities measured by twelve can be made, and a revision of the dozen, shilling, foot-ruler, clock, and calendar may follow at this stage.

Revision of the Measuring Unit 12

Each pair of children has a dozen small articles, e.g., 12 linen buttons; 12 pennies; a foot ruler; a clock face; and a calendar. They place these articles on the desk.

The teacher introduces the lesson by calling attention to these five things used at home and school. By comparing shapes, sizes, uses, materials used in their construction, she points out the fact that they look very unlike each other. She then puts before the children the puzzle which they are going to solve :—

Puzzle.—Find out whether these things resemble each other in any way.

1. The children place the dozen buttons in a line, count and name as 12 buttons or a dozen. 12 pennies are treated in the same way, counted and named as 12 pennies or 1s.

They then look at the ruler on the unmarked side, what is it called ? They turn the ruler over so that the divisions are seen. What are they called ? How many inches in the foot ruler ? Compare with number of buttons in one dozen, and pence in 1s.

They take up the clock and notice the hands and figures. The meaning of an hour is revised. How many hours in a day ? In a night ? How shown on the clock ?

The calendar is treated in the same way, then a summary is made :—

> There are 12 articles in 1 dozen.
> ,, ,, 12 pennies in 1 shilling.
> ,, ,, 12 inches in 1 foot.
> ,, ,, 12 hours in 1 day.
> ,, ,, 12 months in 1 year.

Although unlike each other in shape, size, and material, is there any resemblance ?

2. The result is the same when any of these quantities are divided into 2, or 4, or 3 equal parts.

(*a*) Each pair of children shares the dozen buttons between them, taking one each until all the buttons have been given away. How many buttons does each child get ?

(*b*) The shillingsworth of pennies is shared in the same way. How many pennies does each child get ?

(*c*) The children measure and cut a strip of paper 1 foot in length. They pretend that it is a piece of ribbon, to be shared between the two partners. By folding and cutting, two equal strips are made. When measured, the children discover that half the foot is 6 inches. They compare with the groups of buttons and pennies.

(*d*) They place the hands of the clock at 12 o'clock. They pretend that Mary and Joan are going out for half the day, from 12 o'clock after school. Then they go to bed. How many hours will they be out ? How many hours in bed ?

Compare with (*a*), (*b*), (*c*).

THE MEASURING UNIT 12 (*cont.*)

(*e*) They divide the year into two equal parts, placing the spring and summer months in one pile, and the autumn and winter months in another. How many months in each half year?

Compare (*a*), (*b*), (*c*), (*d*).

3. Summarize on the blackboard :—

> 6 buttons + 6 buttons = 1 dozen.
> 6*d*. + 6*d*. = 1*s*.
> 6 inches + 6 inches = 1 foot.
> 6 hours + 6 hours = 1 day.
> 6 months + 6 months = 1 year.
>
> ½ a dozen + ½ a dozen = 1 dozen.
> ½ of 1*s*. + ½ of 1*s*. = 1*s*.
> ½ of a foot + ½ of a foot = 1 foot.
> ½ a day + ½ a day = 1 day.
> ½ a year + ½ a year = 1 year.

Repeat with quarters and thirds.

Chapter VII

WEIGHTS AND MEASURES

A. Linear Measure

In the last chapter, we considered the foot rule with its subdivisions, inches. A working knowledge of the yard will be required in many of the children's play activities, this must be dealt with when required, and related to the foot and inch measures so that the table of linear measure may be completed.

I. CONCRETE SITUATIONS (See Chapter III)

1. *Goods for Shops.*
   (i) The Toy Shop : Reins and Skipping Ropes.
   (ii) The Drapers' : Ribbon, Lace, Bales of Material.
2. *Festivals*, e.g. Christmas.
   (i) Decorations : Chains, Icicles, Friezes.
   (ii) Party Equipment : Table Cloths, Table Napkins.
3. *Dramatic Properties.*
   Garlands, belts, aprons, tunics, costumes, etc., for plays and pageants.

For all these, the children need a measure. They probably know that material is bought by the yard for they have been to the draper's shop with their mothers and watched the draper measuring out material for a new dress or a hair ribbon. But these facts should not be recalled until the need for a measure arises and the children ask for one.

WEIGHTS AND MEASURES

II. CONCRETE MATERIAL

The teacher then suggests that they show, by outstretched arms, how long they think a yard is, and she goes round the class with a tape-measure, comparing their computation or guesses with the standard measure, noting those children whose length is "*too long*", those who have "*too short*" a length, those who are "*just right*". Strips of cartridge paper, unmarked, and one yard in length are given to the children to be used for the measuring operations in hand, e.g. taking measurements for the dramatic costumes. For measuring skipping-ropes, bales of material, etc., the paper measures should be pinned to the children's desks. It is not long before difficulties arise, the children finding that they need a smaller measure, and the constructive work of costume-making, reins, or draper's stock is put aside, so that a "real" draper's yard may be made.

1. *Fractions of the Yard*

The half and quarter yard will be the smaller measures with which the children have probably some vague acquaintance, and as they will have heard of ½ yard ribbon, ¼ yard lace, these fractions will be dealt with now.

Problem—What do we mean by ½ yard ?
    Compare ½ foot, ½ piece of paper, ½ shilling, ½ a penny, ½ a cake.

Folding the paper measure will suggest itself as the

L

method of finding the ½ yard, after which ½ yard will be printed in each section of the paper.

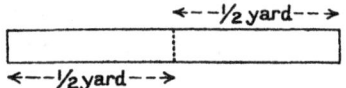

Materials (e.g. lengths of ribbon, wallpaper, etc., previously arranged by the teacher) are then measured by the children. Some are exactly ½ yard. Some are much less, and the children will probably say ¼ yard.

Problem—What do we mean by ¼ yard?
    Compare ¼ foot, ¼ piece of paper, ¼ shilling, ¼ a penny, ¼ a cake.

Again, by folding, the children find and mark in the quarters.

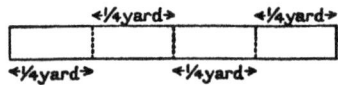

2. *Comparison of Fractions*

By observation of their yard-measures, the children will now find that there are :—

    (a) Two ½ yards in a whole yard.
    (b) Four ¼ yards in a whole yard.
    (c) Two ¼ yards in a ½ yard.
    (d) ¼ + ¼ + ¼ yard = ¾ yard.
    (e) ½ + ¼ yard = ¾ yard.

The children should then return to their work of costume-making, skipping-ropes, or whatever scheme is going forward, and use their measures, again returning to the concrete materials when they find once

WEIGHTS AND MEASURES 143

more that they need a smaller measure even than ¼ yard. The foot ruler already known to the children, is now to be brought into the field for comparison.

3. *Relation of the Foot and Inch to the Yard*

(i) *Number of Feet in a Yard*. By repeating the foot ruler along the yard measure the children find that there are 3 feet in a yard and mark in these divisions.

(ii) *Number of Inches in a Yard*. From the children's knowledge that :—

12 inches = 1 foot, they will readily see, that
2 × 12 ,, = 2 feet,
and 3 × 12 ,, = 3 ,,

Their problem now is to discover the number of inches in a yard. This is done by marking in the inches, and finally, by counting, they arrive at the table :—

1 × 12 inches = 1 foot, or 12 inches.
2 × 12 ,, = 2 feet or 24 ,,
3 × 12 ,, = 3 ,, or 36 ,,

4. *Relation of Inches to Fractions of Yard*

By folding the measures once more into halves, quarters, and three-quarters, they discover the number of inches in ½, ¼, and ¾ yard.

The knowledge should now be summarized. It may be written on the blackboard, and copied into their books by the children.

The Yard

3 feet = 1 yard.
36 inches = 1 ,,
18 inches = ½ ,,
9 ,, = ¼ ,,
27 ,, = ¾ ,,

III. INDIVIDUAL OCCUPATIONS

" Story " Sums

1. The draper sold 2 yards of silk to Mrs. B., and 3 yards to Mrs. C. How much did he sell to the two customers ?

2. Jill bought 6 yards of ribbon. She used 2 yards for her hair ribbons. How much had she left ?

3. Ribbon is 2*d.* a yard. How much would you pay for :—

    2 yards.
    2½ ,,
    3 ,,
    3½ ,,

4. Phyllis bought 2 yards of ribbon for a rosette. It only took 1½ yards. How much was left ?

5. Jack wanted 6 yards of string for his kite ; his father gave him 12 yards. How much was left ?

6. Mrs. Smith bought 12 yards of cord ; after using 8 yards for clothes lines, she gave the rest to Susie and Molly for a skipping-rope. How long was each skipping rope ?

7. Lorna's aunt bought 4½ yards of silk for a dress, and gave ¾ yard to Lorna. How much did the dress take ?

8. If 1 yard costs 2*d.*
    4 yards cost ....
    4½ ,, ,, ...
    6¼ ,, ,, ...
    1¾ ,, ,, ...

9. If 9 inches cost 1*d.*
    ½ yard costs ....
    ¾ ,, ,, ...
    1 ,, ,, ...
    1¼ yards cost ....

WEIGHTS AND MEASURES 145

10. yds. yds. yds. 11. yds. yds. yds.
3 + 1½ = 4 − 2 =
2½ + 1¼ = 3 − 1½ =
2 + ¾ = 2½ − 1¼ =
4 + 1½ = 4 − 1¼ =

B. AVOIRDUPOIS—THE POUND AND OUNCE

I. CONCRETE SITUATIONS (See Chapter III)

1. *Goods for Shops*—Sweets, groceries, greengroceries. Dairy. The Post Office.
2. *Cooking for Special Occasions*—e.g. cakes or sweets for Christmas.

These will be mainly " watching " lessons, for it is not possible to provide ingredients for all children actually to make the cakes or sweets. All can take a turn in finding weights, holding ingredients, balancing the pans, and mixing. The teacher too must watch so that she may discover on what points the children are ignorant, e.g. in one class of 6-year-olds, the principle of balance was not understood, for the children thought that ingredients and weight went into the same pan ! Such misconceptions should be noted and rectified as they arise, the teacher pointing out that the cooking must be finished now, and suggesting that number lessons in the future shall be given to learning about weighing and weights.

II. CONCRETE MATERIAL

Materials—Packets of dried goods of different weights, e.g. haricot beans, sand. Scales, weights—1 lb., 1 oz., ½, ¼ lb. If possible a see-saw or swing-boat.

1. *Idea of Balance*

A swing-boat or see-saw is the best way of demonstrating balance to the children. A child taking her place at one end of the balance will find herself elevated to great heights when the teacher faces her from the opposite seat of the see-saw.

" Why is this ? " is the question asked when the merriment has subsided. " Let us try two children, instead of a grown-up and a child." A big and a little child then enter the boat, and it is noted that the same result is obtained. By contrast and comparison of heavy and light children, the principle of balance is gradually deduced.

The scales are then placed by the see-saw, and the points of likeness noted, after which the children are asked to judge packets of dry goods by balancing them on their hands.

2. *Standard Weights*

(i) *The Pound.*—Children will be asked which tradesmen sell goods by the lb. The grocer's goods will be enumerated, tea, coffee, sugar, beans, peas, etc. Some of these will be on the teacher's table, with a number of weights, 1, $\frac{1}{2}$, $\frac{1}{4}$, 2 lb. From the different weights on the table, the children will be asked to find the lb. weight by comparing with the 1 lb. packets. When this has been found the children may find other lb. packets of goods, e.g. sugar, beans ; loose goods, e.g. beans, nuts, should then be placed on the table, these

WEIGHTS AND MEASURES 147

are to be made up into pound packets with the scales and pound weights.

(ii) *The Ounce.*—The children's thoughts are then directed to the sweetshop, a pound of sweets is weighed, the amount and price noted. At this point a moral lesson can be neatly fitted in as comments are made by the children on the dire effects, gastric and financial. Seeing that from both points of view a smaller weight is advisable, the ounce is shown to the children, who compare it with the pound by balancing on the palms of the hand and on the scales.

Weighing experiences with the ounce are then given— (*a*) Weighing ounce packets of sweets ; (*b*) finding from several packets those weighing 1 oz. ; (*c*) weighing ounces from the loose sweets.

(iii) *Comparison of Pound and Ounce.*—The question next arises—How many ounces of sweets must be weighed before a whole pound is made ? The pound weight is placed in the pan on one side of the scales, and the ounce packets of sweets put into the other pan, so that the children find that sixteen ounce packets are needed to balance the pound weight. From this the children infer that 16 oz. = 1 lb. A ball of plasticene weighing exactly 1 oz. is then given to each child, to model the shape and then stamp it like the 1 oz. weight. The children come up in turns and place their ounce weights on one side of the scales until they find that 16 ounces exactly balance the pound weight which is in the other pan.

(iv) *The Half-Pound.*—Compare ½ penny, ½ foot, ½ yard. Children's knowledge of these quantities will help them to state that the whole pound has to be divided into two equal parts. The pound weight and sixteen ounces are taken off the scales and put on the table in front of the scales. Two children at a time take 1 ounce each, and put it into the two sides of the scales until there are 8 ounces on each side of the scales, and the discovery that 8 ounces equals ½ lb. is theirs! The two lots of 8 ounces are modelled into two half-pound weights, balanced in the pans, and verified by comparing with the brass half-pound weight.

(v) *The Quarter-Pound.*—This can be treated as above, the children knowing from past experiences with the yard, foot, penny, etc., that a whole quantity has to be divided into four equal parts. With sixteen more plasticene ounces, two groups of 8 ounces of ½ lb. each will be placed in front of the scales. Each of these 8 ounces in turn will be divided between the two pans of the scales, so that eventually, four piles of 4 ounces in each will be arrived at.

Four children can then model ¼ lb. weights which will be verified. A blackboard summary of the discoveries should conclude this part of the work.

The Pound

16 oz. = 1 lb.
8 oz. = ½ lb.
4 oz. = ¼ lb.
2 oz. = ⅛ lb.

WEIGHTS AND MEASURES

III. INDIVIDUAL OCCUPATIONS

(i) To supplement the actual experience which the children have had, individual work should make it possible for a few children at a time to experiment with the scales, weights, and dry goods, while the remainder of the class are engaged in other ways.

(ii) " Story " sums, printed on sum cards, e.g.—

1. A parcel weighed ½ lb. How many ounces is that?
2. How heavy will this Christmas parcel be?

    Four ¼ lb. packets of Milk Chocolate.
    Three ½ lb.   ,,   Toffees.
    One ½ lb.   ,,   Raisins.
    One 1 lb.   ,,   Nuts.

3. Harry fetched 2 lb. potatoes, ½ lb. onions, and ¼ lb. carrots. How much did he have to carry?
4. How many ounces make ¾ lb., ¼ lb.?
5. ¼ lb. of sweets and 1 oz. of sweets. How many ounces is that?
6. One parcel weighed 4 lb. 8 oz., another weighed 6 lb. How much heavier was one than the other?
7. Three packets of sweets weighed ¾ lb., ½ lb., and ¼ lb. How many ounces in each packet?

8.

oz.		oz.			lb.	oz.
14	+	4	=	=		
9	+	7	=	=		
12	+	6	=	=		
10	+	11	=	=		
8	+	4	=	=		
20	+	4	=	=		
22	+	10	=	=		
18	+	6	=	=		

9.

oz.		oz.		oz.
14	—	4	=	
12	—	6	=	
8	—	4	=	
16	—	8	=	
12	—	8	=	
16	—	12	=	
16	—	4	=	

C. Measure of Capacity—The Pint, Quart, Gill, Half-Pint

I. CONCRETE SITUATIONS

1. *The Dairy.* Filling milk bottles, cream cartons with pretence milk or cream.
2. *Restaurant.* Filling cups and glasses with "tea", "milk", or "lemonade".
3. *Parties.* Making lemonade and jellies for the dolls' parties. Filling cups and glasses with milk or lemonade for lunch.

Through such activities, the children should be savouring the experiences of those older than themselves, and as the stirrings of ambition are seen in their desire to know how to carry them through correctly, the teacher must be alive to her responsibilities and satisfy desire by definite teaching.

As with the lessons on avoirdupois, so with wet measure, eyes and ears will play a larger part than the hands. It would be ideal for all the children in the class to make the discoveries by actually carrying out the experiments, but this is hardly possible in the large class. The children will have to be content with pooling the experimental work, some actively engaged while others hold a "watching brief".

WEIGHTS AND MEASURES 151

II. CONCRETE MATERIAL

Materials. Quart, pint, gill, ½-pint measures. Pretence milk (water into which whitening has been stirred), spoons, cups, glasses, bottles, cans, and cartons of different sizes.

Ways of measuring liquids will be considered :—
Teaspoon, tablespoon, dessert spoon—Medicine.
Cup and glass—Meals (tea, milk, lemonade, etc.).
Bottles—Medicine, vinegar, oil (for salads), ink, gum.
Cans—Oil, milk in large quantities from the farm.
Cartons—Cream.

Differences in sizes of measures belonging to the same group, e.g. smaller and larger cups, cooking and silver spoons, should be discovered by measuring out quantities, and comparing results. A comparison of the amounts measured will make clear the inequalities and lead to the need for

(a) *Standard Measures*

(i) *The Pint.*—As children will be familiar with this measure, it will be taken as the unit for the milk trade. Children are asked to find the pint bottles from the vessels on the table. Fill from bucket with pretence milk (water into which whitening has been stirred), and label 1 PINT.

(ii) *The Quart.* — Children are asked to estimate number of pints required to fill the larger bottle. After two or three guesses, it will be found by filling the quart from the pint bottles that two pints are required for the quart bottles. The name " quart " is given and a label attached to the bottle. The quart bottle is then placed on the table behind two pint bottles.

(iii) *The Gill.*—This bottle will probably be called the half-pint as children are familiar with that name. The children should be asked, "If it is half a pint, how many of these bottles can be filled from the pint?" The mistake will be discovered when it is found that four bottles can be filled from the pint, and it will be explained that the milkman has still another measure for people who only require a little milk, e.g. small families. This is called the "gill". The gill bottles are labelled and placed in front of the pint bottles.

The children's attention will be directed to the three sizes of bottles now displayed, and the "milkman's table" will be written on the blackboard for the children to copy into their books.

$$4 \text{ gills} = 1 \text{ pint.}$$
$$2 \text{ pints} = 1 \text{ quart.}$$

(iv) *The Half-Pint.*—The children are reminded that they have already spoken of the half-pint. Compare $\frac{1}{2}d.$, $\frac{1}{2}$ shilling, $\frac{1}{2}$ yard, $\frac{1}{2}$ pound, $\frac{1}{2}$ ounce, $\frac{1}{2}$ foot, $\frac{1}{2}$ cake, etc.

The teacher says, "If we have one pint, how many half-pints should we be able to measure from it?"

Two half-pints are found to be equivalent to one pint, and are placed at one side of (though at a distance from) the pint.

(b) *Comparison of Measures*

Recapitulate discoveries made so far. The children

WEIGHTS AND MEASURES 153

know now the relationship between the gill and pint ; pint and quart ; pint and half-pint.

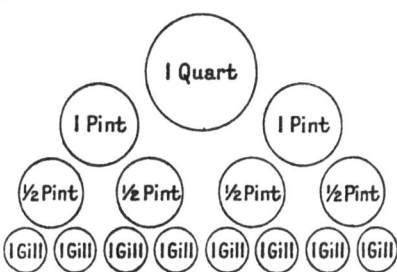

III. INDIVIDUAL OCCUPATIONS

(i) Now is the time for giving all children opportunities for experimenting with the actual measures, for a few children at a time can come out and verify the above discoveries for themselves while the rest of the class can be occupied in other ways.

(ii) *Play in the Dairy.*—A few children can play in the dairy, measuring out milk into bottles, while a limited number of customers come and buy bottles and cartons over the counter. Money and its relation to different quantities of milk will be dealt with here.

(iii) *Play in Desks.*—The children are given cut-outs of quart, pint, gill, and half-pint milk bottles to be used as templates. With their templates, they stock a shop window full of milk bottles and price them, e.g. 6*d.* a quart, 3*d.* a pint, etc. On the opposite page to the dairy window, they make out milk bills for different families.

154   NUMBER IN THE INFANT SCHOOL

(iv) *Further Problems for Children to solve by actual experiment.*

Comparison of Gill and Quart.

(a) If 4 gills = 1 pint, how many gills will be necessary to fill 2 pints?

Children measure and find that 8 gills = 2 pints.

(b) We have here 2 pints or 8 gills.
   We know that 2 pints = 1 quart.
   How many gills   = 1 quart?

Children test.

(c) Comparison of gill and ½ pint
(d) Comparison of ½ pint and quart } These problems can be solved in the same way as (i) and (ii).

(v) *Sum Cards.*—" Story " sums may be printed on cards for the children to solve either by experiment with " milk " and money, or by working in their heads, e.g.—

1. How many pints make 1 quart? 2 quarts?

2. How many half-pints will fill a pint jug? A 2 pint jug? A 1½ pint jug?

3. The milkman sells his milk at 1d. a half-pint glass. How much does he get if he sells 1 quart? 2 quarts? 2 quarts and a pint?

4. Another day, the milkman sells his milk at 1½d. a half-pint glass. How much does he get if he sells 1 quart? 2 quarts? 2 quarts and a pint?

5. A mother has eight children. How much milk must she buy to give them a glass of milk each? How much does she pay if the milk is 6d. a quart?

6. Another mother has ten children. How much milk must she buy to give them a glass of milk each? How much does she pay if the milk is 1½d. a pint?

WEIGHTS AND MEASURES 155

7. Mother took 2 quarts of milk. She made a custard with 2 pints. How much was left?

8. The milkman had 10 quart bottles and 6 pint bottles. How many quarts altogether? How many pints altogether?

9. I have to fill 20 custard glasses holding a gill each. How many pints of custard must I make?

10. In the hospital there are 12 children. They have $\frac{1}{2}$ pint of milk for breakfast and $\frac{1}{2}$ pint for lunch. How many quarts for that ward?

11. For the party ices we used 2 quarts of cream. How many gills did it make?

SUMMARY

Following the lessons on measuring, a talk on milkman's, grocer's, and oil merchant's measures may be given.

Children are shown these measures, they are separated, and the following points brought out in a discussion :—

(a) Shape of vessels—comparisons of density of liquids will lead children to see the use of the lip in the oil-can.

(b) Size of vessels. The milkman's vary in sizes; the very large oil-can of the oil merchant prevents waste, etc.

(c) Protection—stoppers in the oil-can; cork in the vinegar-bottle prevent smell penetrating into the rooms.

Milk-tops keep flies and dust away. Show children gill, pint, and quart measures used until recently.

N.B.—The more hygienic methods of to-day.

Chapter VIII
FRACTIONS
I. Concrete Situations

There were teachers in the past, who, trying to keep abreast of modern educational developments in the presentation of new teaching matter, persuaded themselves that all they had to do—after a few examples had been demonstrated by means of some concrete material—was to make generalizations and formulate rules. When the bewildered children foundered in the trial exercises that followed, the disasters were ascribed by the teachers to the dullness of the children, not to the methods or any mistake on their own part. Receptive and teachable children would have assimilated and turned to good uses, knowledge so ably and intelligently presented!

As an example of such teaching by concrete material, an introductory lesson to a series on fractions may be quoted. Each child, with her own piece of paper, following the teacher's directions obediently folded and cut in halves and quarters, and were told that they had made two halves and four quarters from the whole. This was considered sufficient preparation for a headlong dive into the choppy sea of exercises on fractions in the arithmetic book. But—the teacher might, and probably did, argue—the lesson had been planned on "modern methods" by making use of activity and concrete material, wherein did it fail? So she could only account for all the confusion and mistakes by blaming Fate for saddling her with a "backward" class.

We must again recall the basic truth that "the curriculum is to be thought of in terms of *activity and experience*"; for the educator of to-day, whose work is based on an understanding of sound educational principles, knows that physical activity alone is not educative. Activity, through experience, or concrete situations is the starting-point of all arithmetical processes, and, as we review our scheme, we find that life situations have provided a variety of experiences whereby the children have dealt with numerous calculations involving integral numbers and their fractional parts. Such concrete experiences have been seen in shopping enterprises : in the sweet shop, for example, the whole, half, and quarter sticks of rock have been bought ; sweets, sold by the pound or ounce, may have been made up into half or a quarter of these quantities.

The grocer's and greengrocer's produce has led to deals in dozens, half and quarter dozens ; the pound, half, and quarter pound weights.

In the dairy in the sale of eggs, butter, and milk, the standard measures used have been the dozen, the pound, and the pint, and here again, the fractional parts have been requisitioned.

At the stationer's, birthday and Christmas cards,

and sheets of writing-paper, originally calculated from the whole sheets of paper, appeared in the shop as half measurements ; and then a sheet of writing-paper had to be folded in quarters before it would fit in its envelope.

In all the shops, the whole coins, 1*d*., 1*s*., £1, have been the accepted standards, but occasions have arisen when half and quarter of these amounts have had to be found before a transaction could be carried through.

Sometimes the children have found the need for yards, half-, and quarter-yards, either in the draper's shop, or as they have been making skipping-ropes or dramatic properties ; and the foot-rule, with its fractions, has been required in many activities connected with measurement.

Time, again, measured either by the year (e.g. in their calendars), or the day measured by the hour, with their clocks, has led to considerations of half or quarter of these quantities.

" The end of the exploration is the beginning of the enterprise," and, the teacher, knowing that shortly her little explorers will be leaving the infant school, where they have embarked upon their early quests, will seek to send them on to their next department with the spoils of knowledge, gained through all these experiences, in sure keeping. So she will arrange a series of lessons bearing on simple fractions to clinch and consolidate what they know. Thus will have been formed a background through which they will be enabled to acquire that " working knowledge of the systems of

FRACTIONS 159

notation for integral and fractional numbers—and their written forms "[1] which the primary report includes in its scheme for children above the infant stage.

II. CONCRETE MATERIAL

As an introduction to the study of fractions, a group or class lesson may be taken, the concrete material for which will be gathered together from as many life situations as possible. In this lesson, the aim will be to bring to the foreground of the children's consciousness the meaning of :—

(a) The whole number.

(b) The fraction, as composed of so many *equal* parts of the whole.

(c) The method of expressing the fraction as a symbol in writing.

On account of the impossibility of providing one of each kind of material for each child, it will be necessary to break up the lesson into periods of doing and watching.

Apparatus.—An apple ; one dozen of some quantity measured by the dozen, e.g. buttons, bananas, etc. ; a cardboard penny, a pound note ; a pound of nuts and an ounce of sweets with scales and pound, half-, and quarter-pound weights ; a foot and yard measure made in paper ; a pint of " milk " ; a cardboard clock ; a calendar.

Introduction.—The apparatus, having been arranged on the table, the teacher will tell the children that they are going to repeat the same action with all

[1] *The Primary Report*, p. 175.

160 NUMBER IN THE INFANT SCHOOL

these articles so that they may find out something important which they will need to know in their sums.

1. *The Whole Number.*—The children and teacher will together name each article in turn, *one* apple, *one* dozen buttons, *one* penny, *one* shilling, *one* pound, *one* ounce, *one* foot, *one* yard, *one* pint of milk, *one* clock with the twelve hours of day or night, *one* year with the twelve months.

2. *Meaning of the Term " Half ".*—Two children are called to the front of the group and are asked to share the apple so that each one has the same amount. After cutting it, the pieces are compared with regard to size, and then by balancing on the palms of the hands, a rough estimate of the weight is gained. The children will name each piece as half of the whole, for already they will be familiar with this word. In order to test their use of the term, the teacher will cut another apple into two unequal parts and offer to exchange with the portions held by the children. In this way, the idea of *equal* parts will be brought to the children's consciousness.

3. *The Fraction Expressed as a Symbol in Writing.*—As the children describe the action of taking the whole and sharing the apple, they will arrive at the written symbol. This may be taken in two steps :—

(i) *Drawing.*

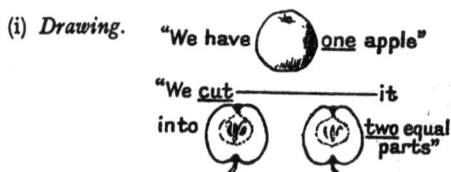

FRACTIONS 161

(ii) *The written symbol.*

The drawing may then be translated into mathematical form.

"We have 1 apple,
We cut————it,
into 2 equal parts."

Each of the articles on the table, representing different standard units of measurement, is then taken in turn and treated in the same way :—

(1) As a whole ; (2) shared or made into two equal parts ; (3) and translated into terms of fractions by writing in the form of a symbol.

In the next lesson, when the quarter is dealt with, the children should speedily discover the method of writing the fractional form. From this, they may pass on to ¾ which they will realize is the equivalent of ½. Finally, ¾ brings the teacher's opportunity for again drawing the children's attention to the written fraction. Already, they know the "cutting" or dividing line –, and the fact that the figure below the cutting line tells into *how many parts* the whole has been cut or divided, should be stressed. By comparing ½, ¼, ¾, ¾, the children should be able to state that the figure above the cutting line tells how many of the equal parts have been written.

III. INDIVIDUAL OCCUPATIONS

With the following shapes, cut in cardboard or paper, the children should be able to—

(i) Find the values of the various fractional parts;
(ii) Find various ways of combining fractions to make the whole;
(iii) Compose their own sums on their discoveries.

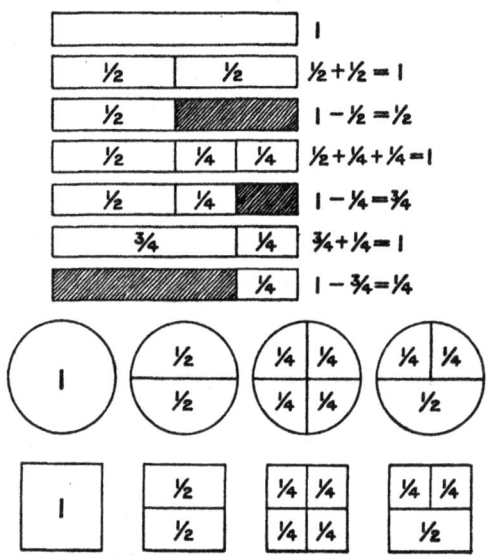

Examples of whole and mixed fractions will be the next discovery, and the children will find many ways of making whole and parts into sums.

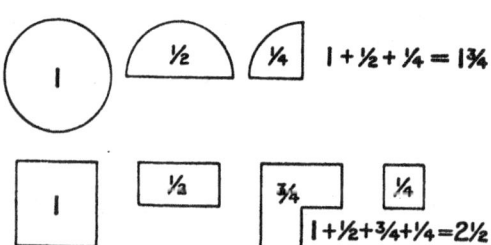

FRACTIONS

$6\frac{1}{2} + 3 =$

$8\frac{1}{2} + 4 =$

$10 + 5\frac{3}{4} =$

$7\frac{1}{4} + 2\frac{1}{2} =$

$3\frac{3}{4} + 1\frac{1}{2} =$

$4\frac{1}{2} + 2\frac{1}{4} =$

$9\frac{3}{4} + 4\frac{1}{2} =$

$11\frac{1}{2} + 6 =$

$2\frac{1}{2} - 1 =$

$3\frac{3}{4} - 1\frac{1}{4} =$

$3\frac{1}{2} - 1\frac{3}{4} =$

$4\frac{1}{4} - 2\frac{1}{2} =$

$5 - 3\frac{1}{2} =$

$5\frac{1}{4} - 1\frac{1}{2} =$

$7\frac{3}{4} - 4\frac{1}{4} =$

$8\frac{1}{2} - 5\frac{1}{2} =$

Chapter IX
NOTATION

Through projects and play-ways, while actually carrying through life-situations involving numbers woven into a systematic scheme, the children will have accumulated a considerable amount of number knowledge. Through experiences ; supplemented by a study of concrete material which facilitates the discovery of principles ; by the application and practice of these principles in individual occupations ; these are the stages by which they have progressed towards the attainment of this knowledge.

Summarizing the knowledge thus gained, we find it includes counting; adding and subtracting small numbers; an understanding of the meaning of "times"; grouping, and sharing. The children know the symbols 1-9, and the mathematical signs +, −, = ; and all this applied to money, weights, and measures. In addition to the scheme, through such other experiences as making calendars, some information has been gleaned about numbers beyond 9. They know for instance that two or more symbols have to be combined in order to write numbers beyond 9.

The aim now should be to *study* numbers so that the children will be able to think, or find out for themselves, *how* to write any number instead of having to ask for the information, and this points to the development of the subject of notation.

I. CONCRETE SITUATIONS

This is the age at which children evince curiosity as to the beginnings of things, and the subject of notation can be approached from the historical point of view. As the subject unfolds it will touch again two fundamental interests of childhood—love of stories and dramatics.

LESSON I. *Introduction*

The children are asked to imagine the district in which they live as it was long, long, long ago—before their fathers and mothers lived and before their grandfathers and grandmothers lived, and before *their* grandfathers and grandmothers, etc. There were no shops, houses, churches, motor cars, trains, 'buses, etc., in those days, for the very good reason that people had not found out how to build or make all these things, for they did not need them. What was the district like and the people? Now pictures of cave-dwellers are shown and their life described.

Story of Richman

Richman was a *very* rich man. But as there were no shops in those days, and no money, because people could get all they needed from their surroundings—fruits, flesh, and skins of animals, etc.—in what did his riches consist?

Picture his flocks of sheep, and how they grew and multiplied, then their life. There was the danger of wild animals by night, and Richman had to protect his flocks by building a sheepfold and seeing that they came home and were safely shut up for the night. At this point the teacher suggests playing a game of Richman and his sheep.

Dramatizing

The fold is made by the closing in and barricading of one corner of the room with chairs; and stones, acorns or conkers are scattered about on the floor. The teacher takes the part of Richman, the sheep-dog's part is played by one child, and the sheep by the rest of the class. The pictures shown of primitive man are left on the blackboards. As the game is played, the following points have to be stressed and made clear: (1) Need for counting; (2) need for a symbol to denote 10.

1. *Need for Counting*.

As Richman has a great many sheep and must know that they are all safe for the night, how is he to tell? The children naturally answer " by counting them ", but when it is pointed out that people did not know how to count, there were no schools and they had not even learned to say the numbers 1, 2, 3, 4, etc., suggestions are asked for ways in which Richman might count. If the children do not think of their fingers, the teacher will remind them of something they carry about with them with which they always count easily. So now they check the sheep entering the fold, just as Richman would hold up one finger as each sheep

NOTATION 167

came in, and in this way discover Richman's dilemma when all the fingers are used up, and this shows the
2. *Need for a Symbol to Denote Ten.*

Sometimes it is suggested that Richman can get over this difficulty by using his toes, but that is vetoed when the children compare the powers of fingers and toes and realize the impossibility of bringing the toes into the vertical position, as they will *not* stand up like the fingers. As the teacher looks around she ruminates and says " Is there anything here I can use to help me remember that all these sheep (shaking in turn each hand with its outspread fingers) have gone into the fold ? " This invariably acts as a stimulus to the children who follow her eyes ; and the stones, conkers or acorns are the materials which suggest a solution to the problem.

A stone is then placed at Richman's feet to remind him that he has " all those sheep " (again signifying the ten by using his hands) " in the fold ".

The fingers now are at liberty to count as another ten sheep are folded, and the game continues in this way till all the sheep are home. It is played several times until a sure grasp has been obtained of the idea, the fingers standing for single sheep and the stones representing one ten, two tens, three tens.

II. CONCRETE MATERIAL

Richman and sheep revert to teacher and children once again, and take their places to pursue a discussion on Richman's methods. The children's attention is

168   NUMBER IN THE INFANT SCHOOL

directed to the counting material and they are asked to explain it in the language of to-day.

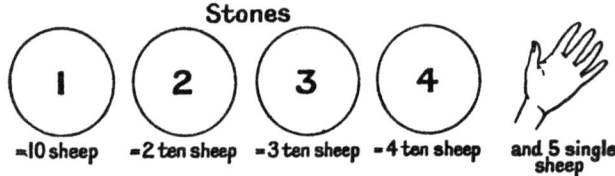

LESSON II. NUMBER NAMES AND COUNTING IN TENS

I. CONCRETE SITUATION

Continuation Story.

The story goes on, and the children hear how hundreds of years later people invented number names —one, two, three, four, etc., to ten, because they had discovered that the ten fingers were useful in counting. They learned to count up to ten, and by tens ; and this was one of the greatest discoveries that the world has ever made.

II. CONCRETE MATERIAL

Keeping to the natural material of the fingers the tens' table will be built up with the children's hands—

```
One child, two hands         = 1 ten
Two children, two × two hands = 2 tens = 20
                              3 tens = 30, etc.
```

The table is quickly and joyously memorized, helped by the rhythmical repetition of -*ty* at the end of each multiple of ten. *N.B.*—There should be no written work at this stage.

NOTATION 169

LESSON III. WRITING NUMBERS

I. CONCRETE SITUATION

Picture Study, Acting, and Illustrating.

After quickly recapitulating the main point in the story of how man learned to count, the teacher should tell the children that now they have to find out how hundreds of years later, people learned to *write* numbers. In preparation for this lesson, the classroom could be divided by chalk lines into three countries of the Ancient World—China, Babylonia, Egypt, each bearing a clearly printed label. The river of each country, can be chalked out on the floor, or cut in a long sheet of wallpaper. On the (i) walls and blackboards of each country should be hung pictures showing typical scenery, geographical features, and natives ; (ii) floor, by the rivers should be the materials which will act as suggestions for writing.

China.—River—palm leaves, cakes of black paint, and brushes in a jar can be placed nearby.

Mesopotamia.—River—damp clay—pointed sticks.

Egypt.—River—rushes (papyrus), brushes and ink nearby.

The children should be divided into three groups ; one group to visit China, the second Mesopotamia, and the third Egypt. Problems are assigned to each to be solved by a study of the pictures.

(1) What can you find out about the country ? (2) The people ? (3) The climate ?

The children return to their places, record their

observations which are further supplemented by descriptions from the teacher of the (i) three rivers ; (ii) vegetation of China and Egypt ; and (iii) geology of Mesopotamia. The history story is continued by the teacher telling of years after Richman lived, there were people in these three countries who knew all that Richman knew about counting and numbers, and so interested were they that they tried to find out what more could be done with numbers.

The idea occurred to different people in each country that they would like to know how to write numbers. " Now," says the teacher, " you children shall again pretend to be these people. Remember that you have no books, no pencils, no pens. You know the names of numbers, but you do not know how to write them. Go back to your own countries of China, Egypt, and Mesopotamia, and when you have found materials suitable for writing, return to your places."

It is not long before the children return with palm leaves, clay, brushes, paint, sticks, etc., after which they will be required to experiment, finding out how numbers were expressed by their use. They will probably set off on strokes as the only method of expressing numbers, but the tediousness of this will be borne in on the children as they try large numbers such as 68, 105. These experiences will help them readily to appreciate man's desire to invent symbols, and they will pass on to expressing in writing the figures 1–9 which they already know.

This should be followed by a brief description from

NOTATION   171

the teacher, illustrated by blackboard sketches of various numerals invented by other countries of the world, so that the children may see that though the idea of using symbols was a common one to intelligent people, yet the methods of depicting them were different in different countries.

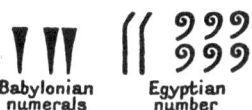

Babylonian numerals   Egyptian number

Again referring to our symbols 1–9, the lesson is concluded by a reminder that as these are the only figures known to us, in future lessons the children will have to learn how people used them so as to make numbers greater than 9.

LESSON IV. NUMBERS BEYOND 9

I. CONCRETE SITUATION

The lesson is introduced by the teacher reminding the children of their purpose, but before this can be achieved they will have to find out all they can about the people who lived in Rome long, long, long after Richman lived; and long, long after people had invented names for numbers and symbols for writing them. To help the children to obtain a correct background for the new work, a description of Roman life, supplemented by pictures, should follow. Great differences in the environment of the Romans, as compared with that of primitive man and earlier civilization, will be noticed for the pictures show

172 NUMBER IN THE INFANT SCHOOL

houses, shops, beautiful buildings, etc. The effect on the lives of the people will be brought to the children's consciousness, that as man achieves more possessions so he will need more knowledge to deal with them. And so we come to the need for schools where we find boys learning lessons, one of which was arithmetic, and the children are told that they are going to learn numbers in the same way as did the Roman boys.

II. CONCRETE MATERIAL

The Calculating Board.

Give each child a cardboard slat 12 by 6 inches (or strip of paper) with vertical lines ruled 2 inches in from the left and 2 inches from the right-hand sides, and a small carton of dried peas, and another of dried beans. Children should be able to suggest how the Roman boys used these boards by recalling Richman's methods—

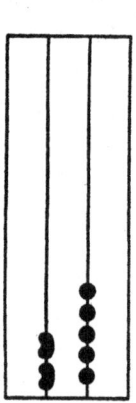

Rich Man

One finger for each object to be reckoned. Ten fingers to be changed into 1 symbol of another kind. Stone, acorn, or conker. Stones and fingers = Tens and single quantities.

The Roman Boys

One pea for each unit required. These to be placed on right-hand line. Ten peas to be changed into one symbol of another kind. Dried beans, on left-hand side. Dried beans and dried peas = Tens and single ones or units.

NOTATION 173

Practice in using the board and material representing the different amounts must now be given.

(a) Comparisons must be made constantly—
    e.g. Place 3 units on the board.
       ,,   3 tens   ,,   ,,

What is the value of each line?
(b) Building up the tens' table.
    1 bean = 10
    2 beans = 2 × 10
    3 ,,   = 3 × 10

(c) The teacher can ask the children to show her a number of tens, then require children to convert these into units.

(d) Our " magic trick ".

The " magic trick " can be played on any grown-up who enters the room, or the children may be encouraged to try it on grown-up friends at home.

Children point to cartons of beans and peas, saying—
    " Here we have some beans, here we have some peas."
    " Can you put out 29 using only 11 ?
                  33   ,,   6 ?
                  24   ,,   6 ?
                  51   ,,   6 ? etc.

In these ways, the idea of place value becomes clear to the children, and they get the practice necessary for " fixing " the principles.

In the same way hundreds can be dealt with, Brazil nuts (or any other dried goods larger than the beans)

174 NUMBER IN THE INFANT SCHOOL

can be used to represent the hundreds which are placed on another line added to the board.

Practice, using hundreds, tens, and units can be given as in suggestions above.

Writing Numbers.

Revise figures known to the children. Children are given a piece of paper ruled in the same way as the calculating board. This is placed in a line immediately below their calculating boards.

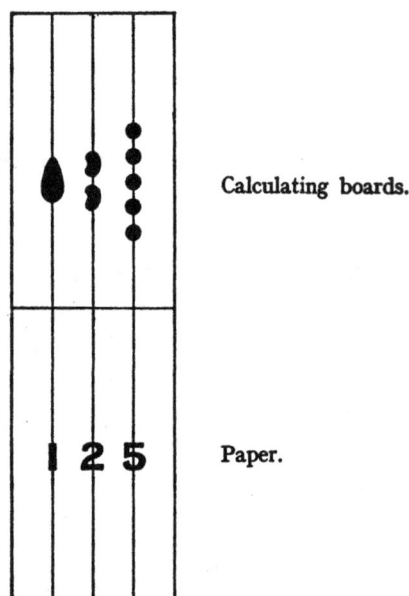

Calculating boards.

Paper.

Children will be asked to represent a number, e.g. 125, on their boards. How many units? What figure will

NOTATION 175

be written to represent the five in the units' column ? Where will it be written on the paper ? How many tens ? What figure will be written to represent the 2 in the tens' column ? Where will it be written on the paper ? How many hundreds ? What figure will be written to represent the 1 in the hundreds' column ? Where will it be written on the paper ? Several other examples will be given.

The Zero.

So far, no mention has been made of the zero. Only invented about a thousand years ago, it appears as a late development in the history of mathematics. In the same way as his forebears, the child is content to pursue his discoveries without any feeling of inconvenience at the absence of the symbol. The time is, however, ripe for its introduction, and the teacher's aim should be to enable the children to feel its lack and the necessity for supplying a symbol representing nothing.

Children are asked to place 20, 30, 40, etc., 200, 300, 400, etc., on their calculating boards, and then write the corresponding number on their papers.

The children will write the symbol for the ten or hundred, but—unless they already know it—they will ignore the units' (or tens' and units') column.

Write the number on the blackboard, and let children write it also on unlined paper. They will then see that, without their calculating boards, they have written a symbol which would be mistaken for a unit. The teacher

176 NUMBER IN THE INFANT SCHOOL

tells the children that the symbol o was invented to prevent mistakes and to make the meaning of their calculations clearer, after which much practice in placing numbers on calculating boards and writing on paper should be given, e.g.—

    20,   30,   40 ;
  200, 300, 400 ;
  150, 270, 380 ;
  205, 608, 109 ; etc.

Writing in Columns Instead of on Lines.

After some practice using the calculating board and paper on a level, the position of the paper can be altered by placing it at the side of the board. The difficulty of reading figures on lines can be noticed, and the children asked to suggest a way of showing amounts by a clearer method. The column will probably present itself to the children, and from this time they should have their paper ruled into columns about ¼ inch apart, and headed Htu.

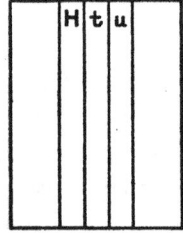

N.B.—Columns should be as close as possible to each other to help the children form the association of 10 as the unit of measurement, as distinct from other quantities, e.g. £ s. d. measured by the 12 and 20.

NOTATION 177

III. PRACTICE WORK WITH INDIVIDUAL OCCUPATIONS

With Tillich's Apparatus.

a. From a box, the child draws a number, e.g. 16. He shows 16 with one ten and the 6 of the Tillich, and places the card bearing the number 16 underneath.

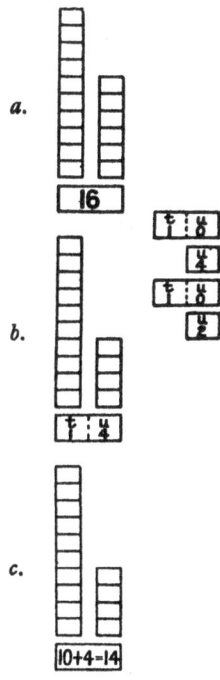

b. The child places one (or more) tens, and any unit strip which he likes on the desk, e.g. 1 ten 4 units. From a box, he finds the ticket bearing the symbol [🕇⋮🖇] 1 ten ; and another unit ticket with [🖣]

4 units. These are placed together under the apparatus to make the number required, 14.

c. The child places any number picture he chooses on the table, and finds from a box the written equation to place under it.

Lotto.

This can be played as an individual or group game. For the former, the aim is to match the apparatus. For group work, the children are provided with cards and the teacher (or a child) calls the numbers from a bag. The child, who finds on his card the number called, covers it up. The aim is to cover all the numbers.

	36		
81		18	

36		9	
	81		18
74		28	
	56		75

Follow my Leader.

0	10	20	30	40	50
1	11	20	30	40	50
2	12	20	30	40	50
3	13	20	30	40	50
4	14	20	30	40	50
5	15	20	30	40	50
6	10	20	30	40	50
7	10	20	30	40	50
8	10	20	30	40	50
9	10	20	30	40	50

[4] [6] [7] [5]

[3] [4] [2] [1]

NOTATION 179

The first column gives the units in order, this is followed by the columns for the tens, twenties, thirties, etc.

The nought is the leader of the first column, the ten of the second, the two tens of the third, etc.

In each column of tens, units have to be found and placed in the correct order.

When the board is complete, the child is able to read the numbers 0–50 in the right order. The child can also write his numbers on paper using his board to help him.

APPLICATION OF THE PRINCIPLE OF NOTATION

Every effort should be made to render more explicit the principle of notation, and to show how it is applied to other quantities in life, e.g. tens and units may be combined to make shillings ; hundreds, tens, and units are wanted to express pounds sterling.

> *A lesson* comparing tens and units of quantities of goods, with tens and units of shillings may be given at this point.
>
> *Apparatus.* Calculating boards, dried beans and peas (or Tillich's apparatus, or bundles of sticks). Imitation ten-shilling notes, and single shillings (cardboard).

Steps in the Lesson.

1. Quick revision—by showing numbers on calculating board, e.g. " Make 12 on your boards ; 15, 17, etc."

2. Quick revision in making up sums of money from 1s. to 19s.

3. The children are asked to show :—

(a) A number, say 15, on the calculating board ;

(b) The same number in shillings.

Several other examples are given. The children are asked to imagine and name goods attached to the numbers represented on the calculating board, e.g. 15 boys, 17 apples, 18 oranges, etc.

4. Comparison of amounts :—

The children place fifteen dry goods on their calculating boards. They compare amounts :—

    1 bean and 5 peas, that is 1 ten and 5 units = 15.
    1 10s. note, and 5 single shillings   = 15s.

5. *Writing the amounts and comparing them.*

The children are given paper ruled into two columns : the left-hand side for money, the right-hand side for quantities represented by tens and units.

	s. t u 1 7		boys t u 1 7

The columns are headed *t*, *u*.

Over the left-hand columns, s. for shillings is written, and a designation, e.g. boys, apples, oranges, etc., is imagined and written over the top of the other column.

Seventeen shillings are represented by the money, while seventeen boys are represented by the tens' and units' apparatus. Each quantity is written in the column provided. A comparison of apparatus and written symbols should follow when the children will notice the similarities of quantities and dissimilarities of materials.

N.B.—The pence column should not be used until after the children have had much practice with the concrete material, and writing of numbers. When they have grasped the underlying idea, they should be reminded of the pence column which was included in shopping bills, after which they may rule the line for the pence column and add the symbol denoting no pence to all the examples illustrated.

s. t u	d.		boys t u
1 7	0		1 7

Notation applied to other Life Situations.

If possible, the knowledge gained should be diverted again into the channels of projects which may be going forward in the class. As an example of such a project, a class of children were engaged in constructing houses for an estate. It was suggested that the houses on the estate should be sold, and an estate agent's office was opened. No house on the estate was to be valued at more than £999, and banknotes of £5, £10, £20, £30, £50, £100, together with the pound treasury notes were given to the children. Sale boards were printed advertising particulars and prices of houses, e.g. £850, £795, etc. Purchasers arrived with pocket books bulging with banknotes, and in paying for their residences, they found themselves involved in complicated counting experiences of a more advanced order, e.g. £100 + £100 + £50 + £50 + £50 + £100, etc. = £450.

The Bank.

From the estate agent's to the bank is but another step in the play for the children, and also another move forward for the teacher's arithmetic scheme. The inadvisability of carrying large sums of money about is realized, and the children readily volunteer the information that banks undertake to keep it in safety for customers. So a new project arises. The class is divided into equal numbers of families and bank clerks. A realistic bank may be made with fireguards propped up on desk or table fronts, behind which the clerks sit with their ledgers ready to receive the customers' savings which are entered into pass-books (by the customers) and ledgers (by the cashiers). Ledgers and pass-books are ruled in columns £ *s. d.* ; the £ column still further ruled into *H. t. u.* As the game develops, a parallel course in number may be pursued by a continuation of notation, with the principles and processes applied also to addition and subtraction of money.

	£			s.		d.		£			s.		d.
	H	t	u	t	u			H	t	u	t	u	
Cheque	4	9	9		0	0							

Page of Pass-Book ruled.

CHAPTER X
ADDITION AND SUBTRACTION OF LARGER NUMBERS

I. CONCRETE SITUATIONS

The teacher of little ones has to remind herself continually of her duty of foresight and forethought for the future needs of the children. In every way, she seeks to prepare them for the larger calls upon their intellectual capital, as they pass on up the school.

Games.—To this end as numbers are revised to include $H.$, $t.$, $u.$, the scoring games (*vide* Chapter IV) may be resurrected, and are gladly welcomed by the children who will attack the old favourites with renewed zeal, after this interval.

Projects. Ships. (*a*) Liners. Finding the number of first, second, and third class passengers.

(*b*) Cargoes. Barrels of apples, boxes of oranges, tinned goods, etc., have to be reckoned.

The Zoo—Records of visitors each day.

The Dolls' School—The doll-pupils must learn to read, write, and do sums, and they may have arrived at the stage when they have mastered all the number known to their teachers. The Doll-School will be closed for the dolls' holidays, and the teachers will learn more " sums " so that they may have more to teach when the new Doll term opens.

II. CONCRETE MATERIAL

A breakdown in the reckoning processes must occur, and as an example of this eventuality, we may take the finding of the number of passengers on liners. The children will be able to write the large numbers, e.g.

>   187 I class passengers.
>   142 II class passengers.
>   164 III class passengers.

but facing the problem of their addition will give the motive for learning to add such large numbers. For this, their apparatus is needed, and the calculating boards and dry goods have to be brought out once more. At this point, it is as well to stress the importance of habit training in early number work. Much time is saved, and confusion of mind avoided, by an insistence on orderly arrangement of concrete material on the children's desks. Before beginning a lesson where this concrete material of hundreds, tens, and units is used, the teacher will be well advised to give directions such as : " Put the carton of peas—i.e. your units—on the right-hand side of the desk," pointing to the children's right hands. " Put the carton of beans—i.e. your tens, on the left-hand side of the desk," pointing to the left hands again. " Put the Brazil nuts—i.e. your hundreds, on the left-hand side of, and close to, the tens," pointing to the left-hand side again. These directions should preface every lesson until the children automatically arrange their apparatus and no longer need such help.

The aim of the new work will now be brought before the children's consciousness, " You could not find out how many passengers you had on your liners, so to-day, we are going to learn to add large numbers, then you will be able to manage."

ADDITION AND SUBTRACTION 185

A quick revision of the history of numbers, methods of showing them on the calculating boards with concrete material, and by writing, will introduce the new process.

Problems and Method

1. *Addition of H., t., u., without carryings.*—Imaginary problems, bearing on the interest which has led to the need for the new knowledge should be given. J. is asked to stand out in front of the class with his liner in his hand so that all the children may see it, while the teacher tells a " story sum " about it.

" J's ship is going to Canada.

In the 1st class, there are 123 passengers
,, 2nd ,, ,, 112 ,,
,, 3rd ,, ,, 134 ,,

Show these numbers on your calculating boards."

The children place the dried goods on the boards, and will be able to total the quantity, 369 passengers. They will be asked to summarize the three operations which they have performed :—

(a) Placing the numbers in lines in their right places on the boards.

(b) Adding all of each quantity together, i.e. all the units, all the tens, all the hundreds.

(c) Naming the total quantity.

Other examples, bearing on the number of passengers travelling by other children's ships will then be given, and the children will rapidly grasp the idea of totalling the different quantities.

2. *Addition of Numbers with Carryings.*—(a) *In the*

Units' Column. Again, using imaginary examples, the teacher should introduce numbers in the units' column.

Passengers.			H.	t.	u.
1st Class	.	.	1	2	5
2nd ,,	.	.	1	3	6
3rd ,,	.	.	1	2	4

How many travelling by M.'s boat? When " Three hundred and seventy and fifteen " are announced, there will be a breakdown. Amazement and amusement will be the children's reactions, horror and surprise the teacher's, as she asks if they have ever heard of such numbers as 3H., 7t., and 15 ; 4H., 6t., and 12, etc., each number being greeted by the children with fresh peals of merriment.

Then, by recalling Richman's story, and the story of schoolboys using the calculating board, the children will remember that only nine units may remain on the board in the units' column ; 10 must be changed into a symbol of the next quantity and leave the odd ones behind. Memory refreshed, and reasoning used in a new situation, the 10 peas on the units' line will be changed into one bean and placed on the tens' line, and five peas will remain on the units' lines. A recount will be made, and the total number of passengers will be found to be 385. Other examples follow, till the children are quite clear as to the conversion.

(*b*) *In the Tens' Column.*—Numbers should now be arranged so that carryings are met with only in the tens' column, and these can be dealt with as in the units'.

ADDITION AND SUBTRACTION

```
H.  t.  u.
 1  4   2
 1  8   4
 1  2   1
─────────
 3 (14)  7
─────────
 4  4   7
```

(c) *Carryings in the Units' and Tens' Columns.*—The third step will deal with carryings in both columns, and by this time the children should have no difficulty in grasping the process.

```
H.  t.  u.
 1  5   4
 1  7   8
 1  5   6
─────────
 3 (17)(18)
─────────
 4  8   8
```

3. **Written Work.**

(a) *Calculating Boards and Papers in a Line.*—" Make haste slowly " is the speediest way of dealing with the

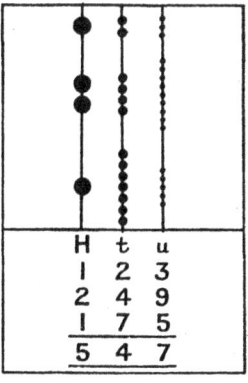

Calculating board.

Paper.

steps in teaching any early number work, and following the same procedure used in learning the principles of notation, the children should begin the written work with calculating boards and papers in one and the same straight line.

At first, the totalling of columns and the change of quantity will be shown on the calculating board, the total quantity expressed by dried goods being simply transferred to the written page ; as in the illustration above.

17 units shown on the calculating board as 1 more ten + 7 units.

17 units shown on the writing paper as 7 units.

14 tens shown on the calculating board as 1 more hundred and 4 tens.

14 tens shown on the writing paper as 4 tens.

5 hundreds shown on the calculating board and writing paper as 5 hundreds.

The children's notice should then be directed to the carrying figure on the calculating board which has been placed in the next left-hand column. How can a carrying figure be shown on the paper ? Three ways may suggest themselves : On the line itself, above, or below the sum. If the children decide to put it *above* the line, it may be likened to someone asking for admittance to a house ; if *below*, it may be someone " left out in the cold ". The next stage in the work is to use this new knowledge in the purpose which was laid aside, when a halt was called to gain acquaintance with this needed knowledge. Individual occupations should also be used as a means of helping the children to perfect themselves in this new process, and suggestions for

ADDITION AND SUBTRACTION 189

these will be given when methods of dealing with subtraction of large numbers has been dealt with.

SUBTRACTION OF LARGER NUMBERS

I. CONCRETE SITUATIONS

Stage 1.

Games.—Comparison of scores in scoring games.

Projects.—Trains, 'buses, and steamers. Number of people getting out at different stages *en route*.

Shops—Selling so many goods from a quantity, and leaving so many.

In many projects and play experiences, the children meet with two kinds of problems which involve subtraction, and it is as well to use both the decomposition and complementary methods in teaching the process until the children realize that there are two ways of doing the same sum, then by experience and comparison they find that one method demands less effort and is quicker than the other. Comparison of scores, in games arranged with large numbers, will give the motive for learning subtraction, when the following procedure may be adopted.

Stage 2.

" *Story* " *Sums.*—As a link between the concrete situation and the abstract work of the second stage, when concrete material apart from a life-situation is used, " story " sums may be made up by the teacher in which the two kinds of problem of taking away and building up are used. The children may follow the stories, doing the workings of the sums on their boards with free illustrations.

(1) (*a*) Mother left 9 lumps of sugar in the basin, Carol took 3 lumps and hid them in a teacup. How many lumps were left in the basin ?

Subtraction by the method of decomposition.

$$9 \text{ take away } 3 = 6,$$
$$\text{i.e. } 9 - 3 = 6.$$

(*b*) Mother came back and found the 3 lumps of sugar. She put them on the table in a straight line (the teacher draws them on the blackboard, and the children on their boards). Mother then went to the sugar-basin and put one lump at a time on the table, at a little distance from the 3 lumps, like this (again illustrated on the blackboard). She now had :—

Subtraction by the complementary method.

$$3 \text{ and } 6 \text{ lumps which make } 9,$$
$$\text{i.e. } 3 + 6 = 9.$$

2. (*a*) Before David went to school, he put 12 marbles in a tin. His little brother took 4 marbles out of the tin and put them in his wagon. How many were left in the tin ?

$$12 \text{ take away } 4 = 8,$$
$$12 - 4 = 8.$$

(*b*) David came back and found the 4 marbles in the wagon. He put them in a row on the table like this (illustrates on blackboard). He then put the other marbles from the tin in a row a little way from the other group, and found that he had 5, 6, 7, 8, 9, 10, 11, 12. Now what has he ?

$$4 + 8 = 12.$$

These trifles must not be scorned as silly futilities. Silly, perhaps, but in the original meaning of the word, " timely, innocent, blessed," the latter especially from the teacher's point of view. And certainly not futile, for by the repetition of these " silly symphonies ", it has been proved to demonstration that the mathematical

ADDITION AND SUBTRACTION 191

ideas in them develop and become strong, healthy growths, indigenous in the soil of the child mind.

II. CONCRETE MATERIAL

Apparatus.—Two calculating boards for each child. Beads of two colours, say red and green, for units. Beans of two colours, say white and brown, for tens.

Introduction.—The children are reminded that they are going to learn how to work sums, which will help them to find out how many more the winner has in games, such as hop-scotch, fish-ponds, etc.

The two methods of working the process, and the steps taken in presenting the new work to the children are best shown by the accompanying diagrams which illustrate the blackboard work of the teacher, and the use to which the children's calculating boards on the desks are put. At each step, it may be necessary to give several lessons, but by following a logical procedure, it will not be long before the children will grasp the fact that the two methods give the same result. They will probably decide that the easier method is decomposition, but the teacher will ask them to suspend judgment until they are more experienced. Later, when fingers are substituted for calculating boards, the children will find that subtraction by decomposition requires more effort, and is a clumsier way of working. Take, e.g. 17–9, the children will find themselves at a disadvantage for they cannot produce seventeen fingers, whereas with the complementary method, they imagine the 9, and fingers are called out to complete

192 NUMBER IN THE INFANT SCHOOL

the rest of the work. When this discovery has been made, it should be decided that from henceforth subtraction sums should be worked only by the complementary method, so that habits leading to speed and accuracy may be formed.

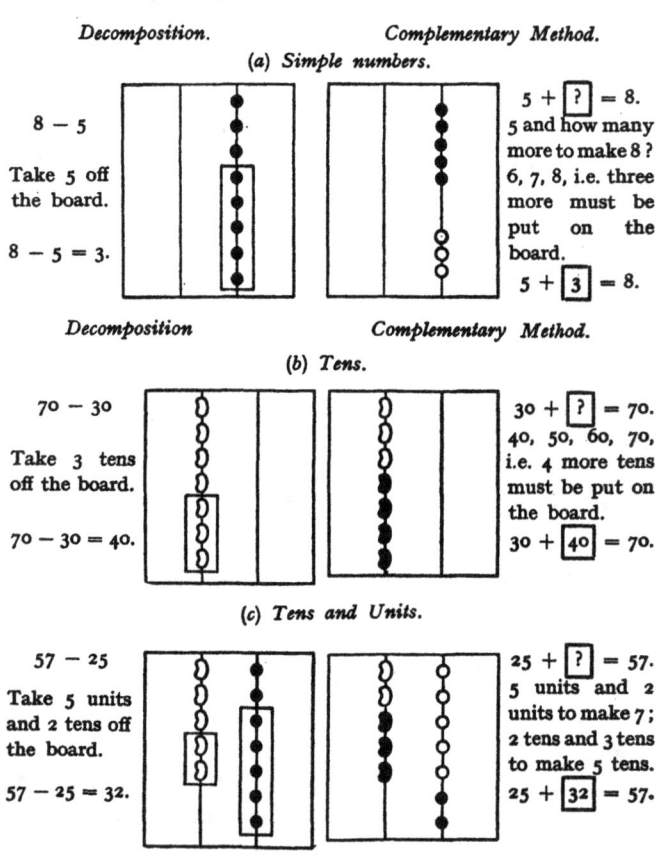

Decomposition. *Complementary Method.*
(a) *Simple numbers.*

8 − 5

Take 5 off the board.

8 − 5 = 3.

$5 + \boxed{?} = 8.$
5 and how many more to make 8?
6, 7, 8, i.e. three more must be put on the board.
$5 + \boxed{3} = 8.$

Decomposition *Complementary Method.*
(b) *Tens.*

70 − 30

Take 3 tens off the board.

70 − 30 = 40.

$30 + \boxed{?} = 70.$
40, 50, 60, 70, i.e. 4 more tens must be put on the board.
$30 + \boxed{40} = 70.$

(c) *Tens and Units.*

57 − 25

Take 5 units and 2 tens off the board.

57 − 25 = 32.

$25 + \boxed{?} = 57.$
5 units and 2 units to make 7; 2 tens and 3 tens to make 5 tens.
$25 + \boxed{32} = 57.$

(d) Carrying Figures.

25 − 18.
Three steps.—
(a) Put 25 on the board.
(b) 8 cannot be taken from 5. Change a ten into units, and so make 1 ten and 15 units. Will that help?
(c) The children will see that taking 8 units from 15 leaves 7 units. Then the other ten is taken away.
25 − 18 = 7.

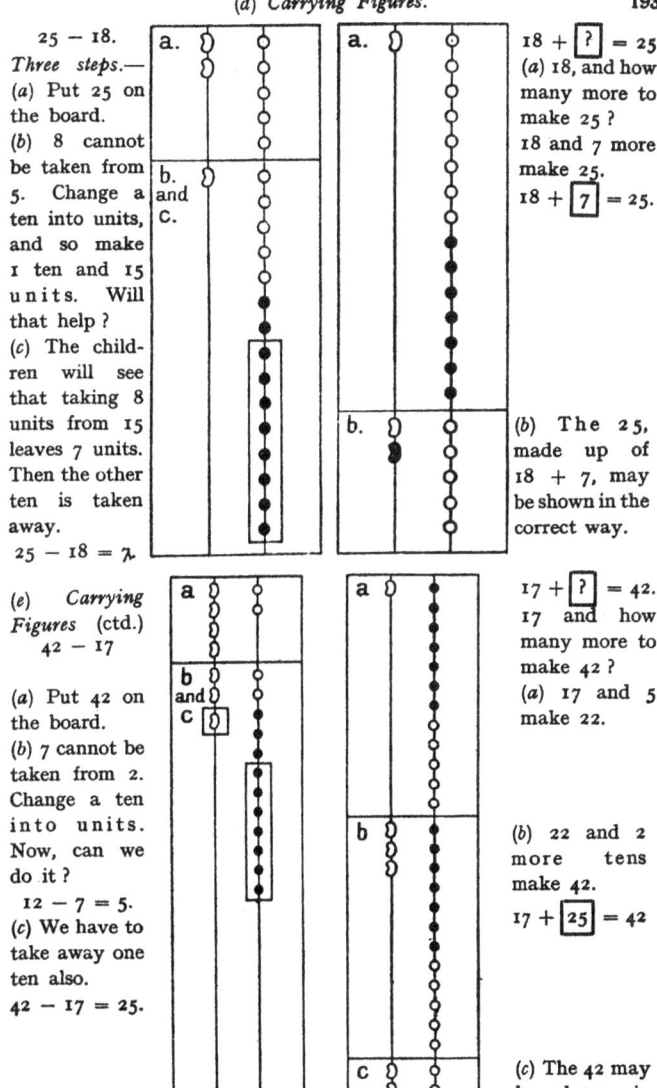

$18 + \boxed{?} = 25$
(a) 18, and how many more to make 25?
18 and 7 more make 25.
$18 + \boxed{7} = 25.$

(b) The 25, made up of 18 + 7, may be shown in the correct way.

(e) *Carrying Figures* (ctd.)
42 − 17

(a) Put 42 on the board.
(b) 7 cannot be taken from 2. Change a ten into units. Now, can we do it?
12 − 7 = 5.
(c) We have to take away one ten also.
42 − 17 = 25.

$17 + \boxed{?} = 42.$
17 and how many more to make 42?
(a) 17 and 5 make 22.

(b) 22 and 2 more tens make 42.
$17 + \boxed{25} = 42$

(c) The 42 may be shown in the correct way.

194 NUMBER IN THE INFANT SCHOOL

(*f*) *Written Work.* $54 - 18 = 36$.

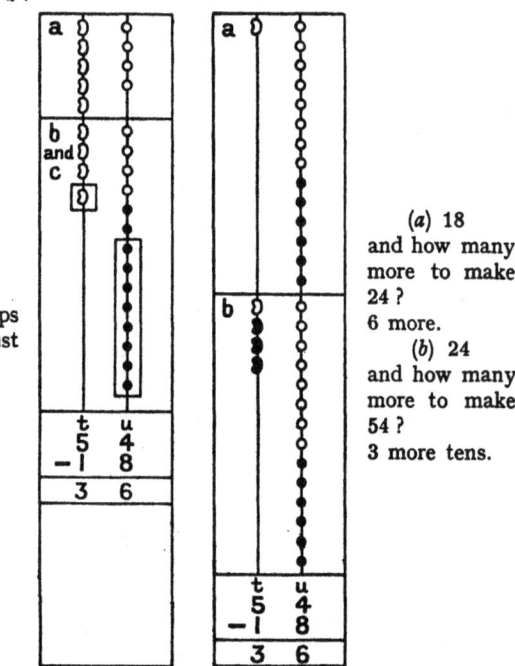

The same steps as above must be worked.

(*a*) 18 and how many more to make 24? 6 more.
(*b*) 24 and how many more to make 54? 3 more tens.

Later, the children say—

    8 and how many more to make 14?
    8 and 6 make 14;
    1 ten and 1 to carry, 2 tens;
    2 tens and how many more to make 5 tens?
    2 tens and 3 tens make 5 tens.

```
      t. u.
      5 4
     -1 8
     ----
      3 6
```

ADDITION AND SUBTRACTION

Written Work in Columns.

As with addition, when the children are found to be ready to work with papers to the sides of the boards, this way may be adopted.

III. INDIVIDUAL OCCUPATIONS

Practice work for both addition and subtraction may be gained with the following individual occupations.

1. *Jig-Saw Puzzles.*

A picture, cut up into various shapes on the back of each of which a sum to be worked is given. When all the answers to the sums have been found, the child

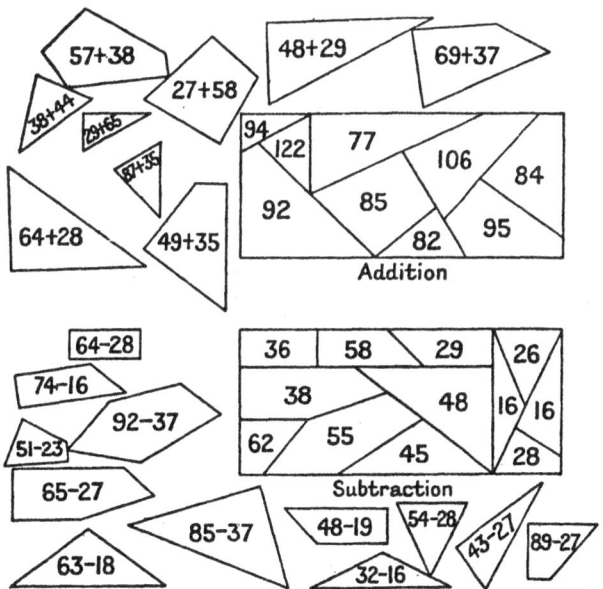

checks his results by finding the correct places on a foreground of cardboard. If his sums are correct, the answers will be found on shapes corresponding to those of the separate pieces, he will fit these on to the board, and make his picture.

2. *Lotto.*

The method of playing this game has already been described in the individual occupations for Notation. The game can be adapted for addition and subtraction.

125		64		129
	61		84	
51		55		82
	73		90	

Addition

75+50=	32+32=
68+61=	45+16=
36+48=	24+27=
36+19=	57+25=
59+14=	58+32=

19		39		47
	36		35	
38		45		18
	54		64	

Subtraction

48-29=	57-18=
72-25=	63-27=
72-37=	86-48=
90-45=	36-18=
87-33=	96-32=

On the loose cards, addition (or subtraction) sums are printed. The teacher (or a child) calls a sum, e.g. 28 + 97. The children work the sum, and whoever has the answer, 125, on his board covers it up. The aim is to cover all the numbers.

ADDITION AND SUBTRACTION 197

3. *Circle Games.*

Addition.—Three concentric circles are cut in stiff paper or cardboard, and joined together with a paper fastener in the centre. Addition sums are written on the cards. The child begins working the first round of sums to the right of the arrow. When he has completed this round, he moves the smallest circle on one place, making another series of sums beginning with 47 + 38 + 49. When this round is completed, the second circle is moved on one segment farther, and when it has come round to the beginning again, the first circle is treated in the same way.

Subtraction.—As for addition, but with two circles only.

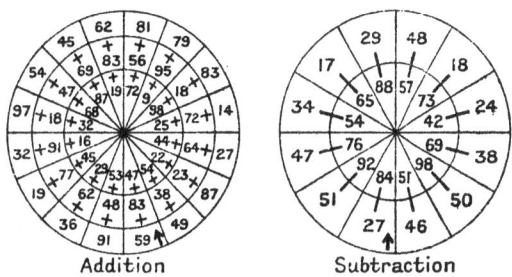

Addition   Subtraction

4. *Magic Squares.*

The children write their own numbers on loose squares. The aim is to arrange the numbers on the board marked in squares so that each line adds up to 50, or 100, or any other number chosen.

5. *Packets of Sum Cards.*

Packets of sum cards, graduated in difficulty, are worked through say from A to E. Each packet is of a different colour, so that the children have the joy of beginning, not only a fresh series, but also a new colour. The sums are arranged in equation form, and have to be transferred into columns, which gives the children practice in place value.

8 + 15 + 22 =	14 + 15 + 17 =
19 + 25 + 15 =	21 + 36 + 28 =
27 + 32 + 14 =	32 + 25 + 16 =
12 + 16 + 24 =	23 + 17 + 18 =

"Story" Sums

1 Peter caught 56 minnows, he put 24 back. How many did he keep?

2. Jim collected 130 conkers, he gave away 40. How many were left?

3. Susie had 125 shells, Timothy found 53 more. How many were there altogether?

4. Lionel had 32 stamps, he bought a packet of 100 and gave away 12 he had before. How many had he then?

ADDITION AND SUBTRACTION

5. There are 125 chickens on the farm, 28 are sold. How many chickens are left?

6. The first form made 162 paper roses, and the second form made 184. How many were there altogether?

7. There were 140 pears on the tree, the wasps got into 18. How many were there then?

8. There are 28 children in the Nursery Class, 50 in the next class, and 47 in the top class. How many children are there in the school altogether?

9. Nora had 110 blue beads. She bought 96 red ones. How many more blue ones had she than red?

10. Pansy threaded 56 blue beads, 72 white, and 45 yellow. How many altogether?

11. Bobby had 144 oranges. Bobby ate 60 and Susie 55. How many were left?

12. Terry picked up 136 fir cones, he put 117 on the fire. How many were left?

1. 31 + 59	4. 13 + 17 + 10	
2. 27 + 83	5. 44 + 55 + 16	
3. 29 + 15	6. 23 + 11 + 4 + 37	

1. 112 + 123	4. 130 + 19 + 51
2. 153 + 145	5. 171 + 125 + 104
3. 162 + 34	6. 15 + 121 + 286

1. 25 − 14	5. 57 − 38
2. 97 − 56	6. 64 − 27
3. 85 − 42	7. 164 − 143
4. 28 − 19	8. 289 − 172

1. 293 − 185	4. 140 − 31
2. 157 − 63	5. 735 − 528
3. 435 − 276	6. 894 − 689

Chapter XI
ADDITION AND SUBTRACTION OF MONEY
I. Concrete Situations

1. *Shopping Activities.*—Situations, involving addition of money, with shillings and pence, have already been dealt with in Chapter V.
2. *The Estate Agent.*—See Chapters III and IX.
3. *The Bank.*—See Chapters III and IX.
4. *Shops with Prices involving £ s. d.*
    (i) *The Jeweller's.*—See Chapter III.
    (ii) *The Furniture Shop.*—See Chapter III.

II. Concrete Material

In their earlier shopping experiences, the method of working simple addition and addition of money has been discovered. The main problem to be dealt with at this stage is the change of unit in each quantity of money used, and much practice with the concrete material—paper Bank and Treasury notes, cardboard shillings, pence, and fractions of pence—must be given before the children can handle automatically and confidently the various units of measure. For in one sum, four units of measure may be used—fractions of a penny have to be converted to pence either by the measuring unit 2 or 4 (according to whether half-pennies or farthings are in question); pence are made

ADDITION AND SUBTRACTION OF MONEY

into shillings by the measuring unit 12; shillings into pounds by the 20; and finally in the pounds' column, a return is made to the 10. This is a great tax on the children's powers of memory, and to simplify the steps in learning and using the knowledge, the following suggestions have been acted upon and found helpful and practical:—

(i) Much experience and practice with one quantity at a time should be given, and not until the children are proficient in using that quantity should another be introduced. See suggestions for bank and estate agent's where pounds' column alone was dealt with.

(ii) The pounds' column. This should present no difficulty, for the children have already dealt with simple addition where the measuring unit 10 is used. No pence and no shillings are added to the other columns, but the children are required to state the total in pounds adding, " No shillings, no pence."

£			s.		d.
H	t	u	t	u	u
2	7	3		0	0
1	2	7		0	0
2	4	5		0	0

(iii) Pounds, with shillings' columns, amounts not exceeding 19s. Much practice must be given in this before requiring the children to tackle the conversion of shillings into pounds. Even though they may be capable of finding the total number of shillings without

202 NUMBER IN THE INFANT SCHOOL

the aid of concrete material, they should be required to show the total with their ten-shilling notes and silver shillings, until they are quite sure that any number from 10s. to 19s. must be written in the shillings' column.

	£			s.		d.
H	t	u	t	u		u
1	2	3		6		0
2	1	4		4		0
1	3	5		9		0

(iv) Conversion of shillings into pounds. Having formed the habit of showing the total number of shillings with concrete material, attention is next directed to the problem of converting shillings into pounds. Much oral work and practice with the money should be given, different numbers of shillings should be placed and totalled on the desk, e.g. 7s. + 8s. + 2s. + 10s. Looking out for the amounts that make, and are changed into, 10s.; in this case 8s. + 2s.; the children are then aware of two ten-shilling notes and seven odd shillings. The two ten-shilling notes are changed for one pound which completes the process.

Eventually, the children derive the rule that columns of shillings are first dealt with as in any ordinary simple addition sum, i.e. by making them into tens and placing the odd shillings under the units of shillings, then a second step—that of putting two ten-shilling notes to a pound—completes the process.

ADDITION AND SUBTRACTION OF MONEY 203

When this knowledge has been gained, and the power to use it acquired, further practice must be given, using pounds and shillings, before passing on to—

(v) Introduction of pence column. Practice should be given in adding up amounts to 11*d*., then the children tackle the still more difficult problem of—

(vi) Converting pence into shillings; and by reason of their former shopping experiences it should not be long before this process is grasped, provided that the concrete material is constantly used at first.

(vii) Addition sums, using pounds, shillings, and pence, may then be dealt with. It is important that the children should still use their concrete material, but if the steps have been worked out in a logical procedure, the children should soon be able to dispense with the cumbersome material of paper treasury notes and cardboard money, and in its place adopt the following simple charts which they can make for themselves.

(viii) Money charts to use in connection with shillings' tables up to £5. A sheet of paper, divided into five equal parts for the five pounds, has drawn in each part two rectangles representing two Treasury notes of the value of 10s. On each 10s. note, ten single shillings are drawn. The amount in shillings of £1, £2, £3, £4, £5 is shown at the foot of each diagram, and the children can quickly find out how to state their totals by referring to the columns, e.g. 6s. + 15s. + 4s. + 12s. = 37s. This amount will be found between the 20s. and 40s., the seven single shillings will be recognized as part of the fourth treasury ten-shilling note, and in addition there are three ten-shilling notes. Thus one whole pound will be seen, one ten-shilling note, and seven single shillings.

Shillings Table.

£1	£2	£3	£4	£5
10/-	10/-	10/-	10/-	10/-
10/-	10/-	10/-	10/-	10/-
20/-	40/-	60/-	80/-	100/-

(ix) Money chart to be used in connection with the pence table. In the same way, twelve shillings' worth of pennies may be arranged as in the accompanying diagram and used in helping the children in the conversion of pence to shillings.

Pence Table.

1/-	2/-	3/-	4/-	5/-	6/-	7/-	8/-	9/-	10/-	11/-	12/-
12d	24d	36d	etc.								

SUBTRACTION OF MONEY

I. CONCRETE SITUATIONS

Shopping activities, the estate agent, the bank, and shops with prices involving £ s. d. as described in the last chapter, will make the children realize the need for learning the process of subtraction of money.

II. CONCRETE MATERIAL

By this time the children should have formed the habit of using the one method, that of complementary addition for all sums involving subtraction, and this method alone should be used when dealing with subtraction of money.

Following the same procedure suggested for dealing with addition of money, the rules for subtraction of money should soon be discovered and learnt.

(i) Much experience and practice with one quantity at a time should be given, and not until the children are proficient in using that quantity should another be introduced.

(ii) The pounds' column. Again, this should present no difficulty for the children have already dealt with simple subtraction where the measuring unit 10 is used, though it must be remembered that the children must be required to state the results of their workings in pounds, adding, " No shillings, no pence " (see Diagram 5).

(iii) Pounds, with shillings' column. Examples of subtraction of shillings without " carryings " should at first be given, e.g. £395 18s. − £179 15s., in order that the children may be aware of the additional quantity with which they are dealing.

(iv) Sums involving " carryings ".

(a) In the shillings' column :—

```
    £       s.      d.
   29       0       0
 - 14      12       0
   _____
```

The first examples will be worked with the concrete material of Treasury notes and cardboard money. £14 12s. will be placed on the desk, and the children will be required to state their problem. How much more is required to make £14 12s. up to £29 ?

The example is worked in the following steps :—

(a) 12s. + 13, 14, 15, 16, 17, 18, 19, 20s. ; i.e. 8s. more to make £1.

(b) £4 + £1 to carry + 6, 7, 8, 9; i.e. £4 more to make £9.

(c) One ten-pound note + 1 ten-pound note = 2 ten-pound notes. So £14 12s. and £14 8s. = £29.

The concrete material on the desk should be arranged as in Diagram 6. See p. 208.

Thus the children will see for themselves that £29 − £14 12s. = £14 8s.

```
    £       s.      d.
   35       6       0
 - 12      18       0
   _____
```

ADDITION AND SUBTRACTION OF MONEY 207

This example is worked in the same way as above, with the additional step rendered necessary by the 6s.

(a) 18s. + 19, 20 ; i.e. 2s. more to make the £, which with the 6s. = 8s.

(b) £2 + £1 to carry = £3, and £2 more to make £5.

(c) One ten-pound note and two more ten-pound notes = three ten-pound notes.

So, £12 18s. + £22 8s. = £35 6s.

And the concrete material should be arranged on the desk as in Diagram 7. See page 208.

(iv) The pence column. The same procedure as in the shillings' column is used in the pence column, the measuring unit 12 being stressed.

As soon as the children are able to dispense with the imitation money, they may substitute simple devices such as those shown in Diagrams 8, 9, and 10, which they can make for themselves. See pp. 208–9.

For the Shillings.

A pound is represented in diagrammatic form as two ten-shilling notes, each showing the ten single shillings. A covering piece is used to find the complement of the shillings dealt with. If an odd number of shillings is under consideration, the notched end A, of the covering piece, is used. For an even number, the plain edge B is used, e.g. 7s. and how many more to make £1 is shown thus :—

7s. are covered with the notched end, and 13s. is seen to be the required amount, i.e. 7s. + 13s. = £1.

14s., and how many more shillings to make £1 ?

14s. are covered with the plain end of the covering piece, and 6s. is seen to be the amount required, i.e. 14s. + 6s. = £1.

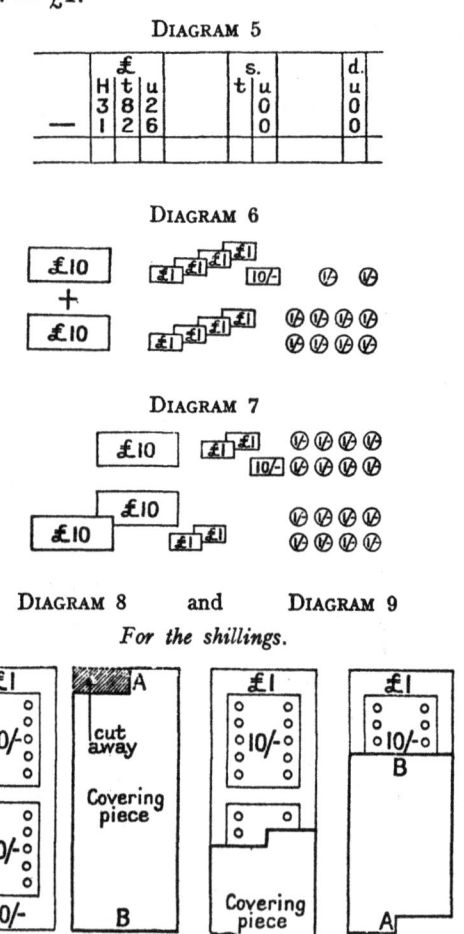

DIAGRAM 5

DIAGRAM 6

DIAGRAM 7

DIAGRAM 8 and DIAGRAM 9

For the shillings.

ADDITION AND SUBTRACTION OF MONEY

DIAGRAM 10

For the pence

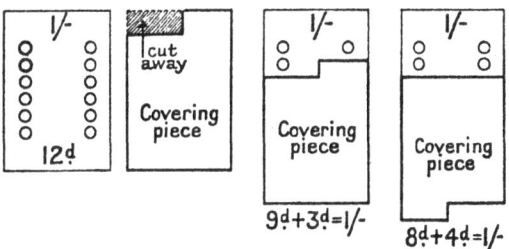

"*Story*" *Sums*

1. Phil spent 2s. 6d. on books and he had 4s. 3d. in his purse, then he paid 3d. for his fare. How much change had he left?

2. Peter's uncle sent him 5s. for his birthday, 3s. for Easter, 4s. for holidays, and 5s. for Christmas. How much was that altogether?

3. Peter had 5s. He spent 1s. on pictures and 2s. 6d. on his sister. How much could he save?

4. The school gymnasium cost £155, the wireless set £30, and the furniture £267. How much was that altogether?

5. In the hospital box there were 16 pennies, 8 farthings, and 6 halfpennies. How much was that altogether?

6. A boy had £2 to spend on clothes. His jersey cost 6s., shorts 7s., mackintosh 10s., stockings 3s. How much was left for his boots?

7. Three brothers bought a bicycle for £3. One

brother gave 15s., another gave 11s. How much did the other have to pay?

1. 1s. 3½d. + 11½d.
2. 1s. 4d. + 9d.
3. 3s. 5¼d. + 2s. 8½d.
4. 5s. 7¾d. + 3s. 4¼d.

1. 2s. 1d. + 7d. + 3s. 2d. + 4s.
2. 5s. 2d. + 3s. 5d. + 1s. 9d.
3. 3½d. + 7¼d. + 4¾d. + 11d.
4. 5½d. + 3s. + 8¾d. + 4s. 7¼d.

1. 6s. 7d. + 4s. 5d. + 10s. 6d.
2. 2s. 5d. + 7s. 3d. + 4s. 6d.
3. £4 1s. 3d. + £2 7s. 4d. + £5 0s. 2d.
4. £5 + £6 7s. 4d. + £3 5s. 7d.
5. £8 10s. + £5 8s. 9d. + £2 1s. 1d.

CHAPTER XII

MULTIPLICATION TABLES

I. CONCRETE SITUATIONS

Many and varied experiences in dealing with " times " have been afforded to the children throughout their infant school career. In their shop plays, they have paid for their fruit and other goods, one 2*d*., two twopences, three twopences ; one 3*d*., two threepences, three threepences, etc. ; 'bus tickets have been grouped in twelves of each price by the 'bus conductors. In learning to tell the time, they discovered that each of the twelve hours is made up of twelve groups of five minutes ; and, as they had recourse to the yard measure, they found it contained 3 feet, or three groups of 12 inches.

In the making and arranging of sheets of stamps to the value of 1*s*. for their post office, yet another demonstration of the tables has been given.

Out of these different " industrial " situations, incidental experiences involving different numbers have cropped up, and the idea of " times " has been brought into prominence. The impressions made on the children's minds have been clear-cut and deep because they sprang up and developed out of real and living needs, so that now the children should be ready to systematize all this knowledge and translate it into the language of the mathematician. To this end, and

212 NUMBER IN THE INFANT SCHOOL

as a link between the stage when the situations dealt with are purely concrete and the abstract stage, the children might make an illustrated table-book. A small, oblong book has one side of each pair of pages used for the picture, with the table facing it on the opposite page. On the picture page, the illustrations of the table are taken from some unit which shows in its composition the number of parts of the table in question, e.g. the clover-leaf, with its three divisions is seen as one group of three; two clover leaves, each with three leaflets—two groups of three, etc.

From the pictures of the clover leaves, arranged in groups, the table will be built up on the right-hand side of the book, thus :—

$$
\begin{array}{l}
1 \times 3 = 3 \\
2 \times 3 = 6 \\
3 \times 3 = 9
\end{array}
$$

Examples of Pictures which might be used for a table-book.

Pairs of gloves, shoes, etc.　　　　　　　　　Twice.

Clover leaves.　　　　　　　　　Three times.

Maltese Cross.　　　　　　　　　Four times.

MULTIPLICATION TABLES 213

Fingers on the hand.   Five times.

Sixpence.   Six times.

The school term is 12 weeks.   Seven times.

$1\frac{1}{2}d.$ stamps.   Eight times.

Stamps for parcels (2–5 pounds).   Nine times.

A pair of hands.   Ten times.

Tillich's Apparatus.   Eleven times.

Dozens, shilling, foot ruler.

Twelve times.

II. CONCRETE MATERIAL

Tables, having been motivated and systematized, it is usual to find that interest has been transferred from the interest in situations inspired by life, to interest in the purely mathematical side of the work. It is now the teacher's duty in this intermediate stage to forge a connecting link between the concrete and the abstract, and for this, various forms of concrete material may be used.

1. Conkers, acorns, beads, counters, or any other cheap and easily procured material will help to an understanding of the principles of the multiplication table, and make clear in the children's minds the table in its two forms.

Choosing a table which holds a special place in the children's affections (for children have favourites in tables, and at this stage it is not necessary to keep rigidly to a logical order), the children are told that they are going to find out something amusing about the tables. With their material, they are asked to show 2×4, and two groups of 4 are set out on the desk. They are then asked to break up the groups into twos, and they find that they now have 4×2. 3×4 is shown as 3 groups of 4, and then broken up into four groups of three, after which other examples

MULTIPLICATION TABLES 215

from the table are taken, until the children grasp the fact that the formula may be expressed in two ways, e.g. 6 × 4 = 4 × 6.

The teacher who would avoid the mistake so often made in the early stages of number teaching, recalls and practises the golden rule, " Make haste slowly " ; and, discouraging hasty generalizations from just a few examples, urges the children to apply the test to the other tables. Then, by pooling the results arrived at by individual children, the rule may be confirmed and established, and a new table book compiled with the tables in the two forms.

1 × 7 = 7	7 × 1 = 7
2 × 7 = 14	7 × 2 = 14
3 × 7 = 21	7 × 3 = 21
4 × 7 = 28	7 × 4 = 28
5 × 7 = 35	7 × 5 = 35
6 × 7 = 42	7 × 6 = 42
7 × 7 = 49	7 × 7 = 49
8 × 7 = 56	7 × 8 = 56
9 × 7 = 63	7 × 9 = 63
10 × 7 = 70	7 × 10 = 70
11 × 7 = 77	7 × 11 = 77
12 × 7 = 84	7 × 12 = 84

2. *A Table Square.*—The construction of a table square will act as a mental stimulus, as it helps the children to understand the principle underlying the structure of the multiplication tables. For practical purposes it is a great help, by enabling the children to see at a glance the whole table, also it occupies only a very small space.

A square, marked off in smaller squares, 12 × 12, is given to each child. Across the top, and down the left-hand side, the children write the numbers 1–12. Each table is then built up in turn, the children being encouraged to verify the results by counting the groups of squares which give the required products. Table square complete, the children prove its value in that it enables them to recover quickly the tables which have escaped from memory, e.g. 9 × 8, the multiplier is found in the left-hand column, the multiplicand in the top column, and, running the fingers along the lines, they meet in the square 72, which gives the product required. This can also be tested by reference to the lines of squares, e.g.—

1 line of 9 squares = 9 squares,
2 lines of 9 squares = 18 squares,
3 lines of 9 squares = 27 squares, etc.

1	2	3	4	5	6	7	8	9	10	11	12
2	4	6	8	10	12	14	16	18	20	22	24
3	6	9	12	15	18	21	24	27	30	33	36
4	8	12									
5	10	15									
6	12	18									
7	14	21									
8	16	24									
9	18	27									
10	20	30									
11	22	33									
12	24	36									

III. INDIVIDUAL OCCUPATIONS

Experience gained through concrete situations;

Knowledge consolidated through concrete material; it now remains for

Power to clinch experience and knowledge.

This most important part of the work must not be neglected, for no child can afford to be without the multiplication tables. By this time, many of the

MULTIPLICATION TABLES

tables should be safely lodged in memory, but quick automatic responses are necessary before the tables can be said to be fixed ; and now practice with individual occupations, such as the following, may be given.[1]

1. *Jig-saws.*

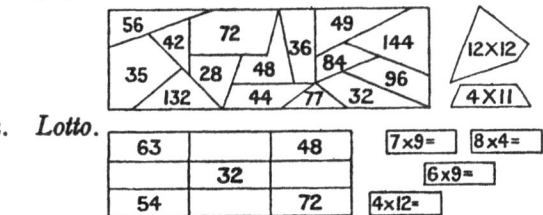

2. *Lotto.*

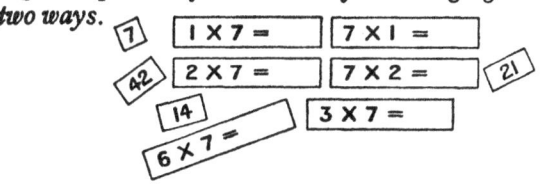

3. *A packet of loose cards for arranging the table in two ways.*

4. *Table Slats.*—The pairs are printed on a strip of cardboard, and the product on another. These may be arranged in three ways :—

(*a*) The children arrange the slats in order on the desks, and then find each corresponding product.

(*b*) Each child has, and arranges on the desk, slats bearing the pair of numbers of the table. She picks up one of her slats and runs to the front of the room where is placed a table on which the products are scattered. Search must be made for the required product, and the child then returns to her place and fits the two pieces together.

[1] The mechanization will not necessarily be perfected before the age of 8 or 9. See *Primary Report*, pp. 175, 176.

218 NUMBER IN THE INFANT SCHOOL

(c) Each child has, and arranges, a number of the slats giving the answer on her desk. The teacher holds the corresponding slats and calls a pair, say 4 × 6. Whoever calls the answer first, pairs and keeps the cards.

9 × 9 =	81
12 × 11 =	132
7 × 8 =	56

5. *Clock Face.*—The numbers 1, 2, 3, 4, 5, 6 ... 12 are written round the circumference. Figures 2–12 are printed on round pieces of cardboard, one of which (the table to be practised) is pinned on to the centre, e.g. 5. The teacher points to the numbers round the clock face, and the children find five times each number as she points.

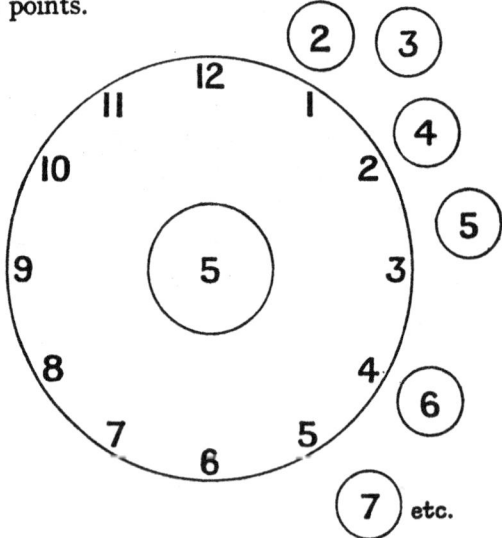

Chapter XIII
MULTIPLICATION AND DIVISION
1. Concrete Situations

Throughout their Infant School career, the children have encountered "times" constantly under many guises. In arranging and grouping articles for constructive or play experiences, e.g. in chain-making for Christmas decorations; arranging 6d. and 1s. worth of pennies in twos or threes; counting the groups of five minutes round the twelve hours of the clock, etc. —each activity has contributed so much valuable grist for the mathematical mill, and its cumulative effect will be felt now the time has come for a clear understanding of the term.

The underlying principle of the "times" concept has been discovered by now in the building up of tables, and will be required in the next process to be studied in the systematic order of the Number scheme —the working of multiplication sums. Before this can take place, however, situations directly giving rise to the need for learning multiplication should be arranged in connection with the children's play activities.

1. The (teacher) shopkeeper, again a very far-sighted being, prepares for a trade revival, and orders from a wholesaler—

12 boxes of oranges with 24 in each box
18 ,, ,, apples ,, 36 ,, ,,

2. Or, as head mistress of the flourishing dolls' school, she has a long requisition list to send for so many boxes, each containing a gross of pencils, packets of twenty-five exercise books, etc.

The children will see the need for starting factories, warehouses, educational supply stores to meet these demands of the various dealers, and there will be a big boom in play activities.

3. The bulb farm, another enterprise, started by the Dutch farmer, offers fresh problems. Fifteen beds to be planted with fifty-four bulbs (of brown paper "planted" in holes bored in the lids of dress or other cardboard boxes)!

Any of these situations will show the children their ignorance, and play activities will be abandoned so that they may learn how to deal with the problems crowding in on their minds and frustrating progress.

II. Concrete Material

Drawing is the best medium for discovering the method of dealing with this process of multiplication.

Take the example of the Dutch farmer requiring to know how many bulbs he wants if he is going to plant fifty-four in each of eighteen beds. The drawing may be represented thus, the oblongs standing for the beds, and the figures for the bulbs :—

| 54 | 54 | 54 | 54 | 54 | 54 | 54 | 54 | 54 | 54 | 54 | 54 | 54 | 54 | 54 | 54 | 54 | 54 |

The difficulty of this form will be realized when the

MULTIPLICATION AND DIVISION 221

children are asked to find the total, and the alternative method of drawing the beds in the vertical plane will be substituted :—

```
54
54
54
54
54
54
54
etc.
```

"Add the columns," will be the children's suggestion for finding the total number, and, beginning with the units, they will add the fours together—

$4 + 4 = 8 + 4 = 12 + 4 = 16 + 4 = 20$, etc.

Repeated addition is thus the first step towards the understanding of the abstract work of dealing with the process, but it will not be long before the children recognize that tables are being used in their calculations, and then they may choose to find 12×4, and add on all the other fours.

Other examples should be worked in the same way before the children's attention is directed to the extravagance of this method, both with regard to time and paper, though the children may not regard this as detrimental. They may agree with the sentiments of one little girl who expostulated, "But I like long sums. I like to use a lot of paper for my sums!"

To lead on to multiplication proper, we may take another "story sum". How many bulbs will the farmer require if he is going to plant 59 in each of 12 beds?

Dividing the blackboard into two columns, the example is first worked as repeated addition in the left-hand column. The children are then asked for suggestions for shortening the sum. " Need we write 59 each time ? " asked one teacher. " We might put ditto for all but the first 59," said one bright little girl. This idea was adopted, the teacher rubbing out and replacing eleven of the 59's by the ditto sign. In this way, the clue was given, and the children saw the necessity for writing 59 once, and for 12 times 59. By reference to the table form, the complete statement 59 × 12 was arrived at, the teacher only having to show how the multiplier is placed under the multiplicand in order to simplify the sum.

After working such an example by multiplication in the right-hand column, a discussion comparing the two methods follows.

```
t.u.
59              59 × 12
59              12
59              —
59              —
59
59
59
59
59
59
59
50
—
—
```

MULTIPLICATION AND DIVISION 223

Other examples should be worked by both methods, after which repeated addition may be dropped and the multiplication form permanently adopted.

III. INDIVIDUAL OCCUPATIONS

The suggestions given for multiplication tables in the last chapter can be adapted for the practice work necessary for multiplication.

" Story " Sums

1. There are 3 boxes of tangerines with 12 in each box. How many tangerines are there in the three boxes?

2. I bought 4 boxes of figs with 18 in each box. How many figs are there in the 4 boxes?

3. There are 5 flower beds with 26 plants in each. How many plants are there in the 5 beds?

4. There are 12 doors in the house and 8 screws in each handle. How many screws in all the doors?

5. There are 28 beds in the hospital ward, and every bed has 4 castors. How many castors are there in the ward?

			s.	d.
1.	22 × 7 =	1.	1	3 × 3
2.	31 × 3 =	2.	2	5 × 2
3.	25 × 2 =	3.	4	3 × 3
4.	45 × 5 =	4.	2	$2\frac{1}{4}$ × 4
5.	72 × 7 =	5.	3	$6\frac{1}{4}$ × 3
6.	15 × 9 =	6.	5	$6\frac{1}{2}$ × 6
7.	83 × 6 =	7.	3	$7\frac{1}{4}$ × 3
8.	46 × 12 =	8.	6	$8\frac{1}{4}$ × 2
9.	51 × 11 =	9.	4	$3\frac{1}{4}$ × 5

DIVISION

Life to the full has been the happy lot of the denizens of the infant school, where the curriculum is planned to work itself out " in terms of activity and experience rather than of knowledge to be acquired and facts to be stored ". Nearing the end of this stage, the teacher will probably review the children's careers, and recount their numerous experiments and rejoice in the diversity of them. In learning " how to live ", they have dealt with those things which have an immediate value for them, gleaning a rich harvest of ideas which have directly helped them " to strengthen and enlarge their instinctive hold on the conditions of life by enriching, illuminating, and giving point to their growing experience " (Primary Report, p. 93).

As we have traced the development of the mathematical side of the child's education in the infant school, we have seen that *experience* paves the way for *knowledge*, desire for *knowledge* leads to *understanding of principles*, and the good work is rounded off and completed by the wholesome discipline of *memory*, which gives the child added power and releases him for further adventures in living.

Throughout these years of complete living, the teacher has duly appreciated the children's experiences and used them to dovetail into a systematic scheme of number work. Now, she recalls the various situations in which the children, when seeking solutions to their problems, have had recourse to the two different,

MULTIPLICATION AND DIVISION 225

though closely allied, interpretations of division—measuring and sharing.

As they have launched upon co-operative play enterprises for which quantities of goods have been made, they have grouped these according to some measure fitted to the quantity under consideration. It may have been the arrangement of the sweets sold by the box in the sweet-shop business. Taking the case of 36 chocolates arranged in lines of 4—this is the child's way. First, he takes four chocolates away from the whole number, arranging them in a line ; then he proceeds to take a second, a third, a fourth, a fifth, and finally a ninth group, placing each in line in the box. This work accomplished, the child finds that 36 chocolates are placed in 9 lines of 4, and the box is ready for sale. In the language of the mathematician, this has been an experience in " Division by Measuring ", i.e. the discovery has been made that 36 can be measured 9 times, with 4 as the measuring unit ; or, in mathematical symbols, the statement would read thus :—

36 sweets ÷ 4 sweets = 9 sweets.

On still another occasion the business in hand may be the stocking of the haberdashery department of the draper's shop for which cards of buttons have to be prepared. These cards are divided lengthways in half, and again widthways into quarters, and the total quantity of buttons to be shared between the four partitions is 24. The child places one button in each section of the card and repeats the operation until all the buttons are safely housed when it is found that there are six in each part of the card. This, the mathematician would say, is an example of " Division by Sharing ", for in sharing up the 24 buttons amongst the four parts of the card, one quarter of the quantity is found, which is the result of dividing 24 into four equal parts.

A leaf now taken from the teacher's record book may serve to show that a number of concrete experiences has been accumulated whereby the children have been introduced to these two operations included under the term division : division by measuring, and division by sharing or fractional division.

Division by Measuring

The Sweet Shop.—Sweets, sold by the box, arranged in lines of a certain number.

The Greengrocer's.—Quantities of fruit arranged in boxes or baskets, so many of the fruit to a box or basket.

The Stationer's.—So many sheets of writing paper, so many envelopes, made into packets each containing so many of the quantity under consideration. So many post cards to be made into elevens.

The Flower Shop.—Flowers made into bunches of 3, 6, 10, 12.

'Bus or Tram Tickets.—So many tickets arranged in dozens according to their values.

Christmas Preparations.—Making crackers and dividing them into boxes, so many in a box.

Lunch or Party Equipment.—The total number of

MULTIPLICATION AND DIVISION 227

plates or table napkins made by the whole class, is made up into packets of 6, 8, 10, 12.

The Zoo.—Entrance tickets are made into rolls, so many in each roll. Biscuits for the animals (modelled from clay or dough) made into packets of 6, 8, 10, 12.

Division by Sharing

The Draper's Shop.—The haberdashery department as above.

Christmas Decorations.—Packets of coloured strips for chain-making shared equally among a group of say, four children.

Dramatic Properties.—Garlands for May Day—so many flowers are made and shared amongst so many children in preparation for making them up into garlands.

The Dairy.—Boxes of cheese are divided into so many equal parts, e.g. 4, 6, 8, 12.

So varied should the children's play life have been that they will have met with these two operations, and be familiar with the significance of each by the time that they come to the serious study of the process of division, and the teacher might arrange her series of lessons on the subject as follows.

I. DIVISION BY MEASURING

1. CONCRETE SITUATIONS

1. The need for a thorough overhaul and tidying-up in the stationery cupboard, served one teacher as a

good introduction to her course of lessons on division by measuring. Inviting the children's co-operation, and stirring their spirits within them, by a comparison of the boxes of loose pencils, india rubbers, and chalks with the orderly arrangements of those other boxes fresh from the manufacturer's, the teacher's double-edged purpose was soon well on its way to fulfilment. For the children quickly set to work to emulate the manufacturer's far better ways, and soon pencils were being arranged in dozens, rubbers in sixes, and chalks in eights. After they had feasted their eyes on the neat cupboard, the result of their own planning, they returned to the schoolroom and heard without surprise that they had been " doing sums ", for by this time they had come to regard sums as bound up with life and reality. They knew that the finished results of their labours had shown them their tables, for they had arranged 12×12 pencils, 9×8 rubbers, and 6×12 pieces of chalk. But when asked by what process they had arrived at these tables, they could not reply. This was indeed the psychological moment for *learning*, and enthusiasm being red hot, the teacher struck.

2. Making up and illustrating " story sums " was the next step in this first stage of learning, and examples, such as the following, were used to lead the children from reality to the abstract work.

(i) A shopman had 32 Easter eggs which he put in little baskets. How many baskets did he fill if he put 4 in each basket ?

MULTIPLICATION AND DIVISION

This was worked by the following steps:—

(*a*) Drawing 32 Easter eggs.

(*b*) Drawing the 32 eggs in groups of 4.

(*c*) Encircling the groups of eggs by drawings of baskets.

(*d*) Counting the number of baskets.

(*e*) Converting the drawings into " sum " form. By examining their drawings, the children translated them into symbols thus:—

    32 represented the whole quantity of eggs.
    4 represented the number in each group.
    8 represented the number of baskets.

All that remained for the children to be told was the conventional symbol, which they now understood as showing what had been done with the eggs.

$$32 \div 4 = 8.$$

(ii) Forty-five roses were tied into bunches, 5 in each bunch. How many bunches were made?

(*a*) The drawings.

(*b*) The statement—45 roses tied into bunches of 5 = 9 bunches.

(*c*) The written formula—45 ÷ 5 = 9.

II. CONCRETE MATERIAL

1. It will not be long before the children realize the relationship existing between the multiplication tables and this new process, and thoughts may be directed to the concrete material of the table square. Choosing from it any examples they like, the children will find much exhilaration in writing them on the left-hand side of their books, and giving them in their converse form on the right-hand side.

$$7 \times 8 = 56 \qquad 56 \div 8 = 7$$
$$6 \times 9 = 54 \qquad 54 \div 9 = 6$$
$$8 \times 3 = 24 \qquad 24 \div 3 = 8$$

MULTIPLICATION AND DIVISION

2. *Division of Tens and Units.*—Following on from this work with tables, division with larger numbers must be attacked, and Tillich's apparatus will be found invaluable as concrete material in this connection.

(i) 64 ÷ 2.

Six tens and a four are arranged on the desk, from which the children will see that their problem is to find how many twos there are in sixty and how many twos in four. As the quantity is to be measured by a two, the tens are then placed in twos with a small space between each pair. The child takes up a 2 from his box of apparatus, and, using it as a measure, places it across the first pair of tens and finds that the first pair of tens yields 10 twos; then on to the second, which, with the first gives twenty twos; then on to the third pair and arrives at 30 twos, and eventually he discovers that 60 contains 30 twos. Then, measuring the 4 by 2, he finds 2 twos, a familiar friend.

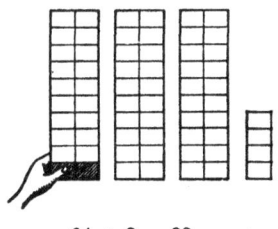

64 ÷ 2 = 32

And the other way of writing this is shown :— $\frac{32}{2)\overline{64}}$

(ii) 56 ÷ 4, i.e. 56, is to be measured by 4.

Arranging the apparatus as 4 tens + 1 ten + 6, the

children measure *across* the 4 tens with their unit of measure 4, when they find that the 4 tens contain 10 fours. The remaining 10 and 6 = 16, and is found to contain 4 × 4.

$$\text{So, } 56 \div 4 = 10 + 4 = 14,$$
$$\text{or, } \quad 4\overline{)56}^{\,14}$$

After numerous trials (for children must be guarded against the common error of generalizing from one or two instances) the children may pass on to Stage III.

III. INDIVIDUAL OCCUPATIONS

Cards of "story" sums are given to the children, e.g.—

1. The children in a school bought 125 bulbs. They planted them 5 in a pot. How many pots did they plant?

2. The dairyman packed 288 eggs in boxes that held 6 each. How many boxes were packed?

3. There were 288 crackers to be packed in boxes by putting 12 in a box. How many boxes would be needed?

4. The cook washed up 108 plates and she put 12 plates in a pile. How many piles of plates would be on the dresser?

5. Father was building a garden wall. He had 420 bricks and he asked the boys to bring them six at a time. How many times would they have to come?

6. The gardener has 36 bulbs to plant and puts 4 in a pot. How many pots must he have?

MULTIPLICATION AND DIVISION 233

7. The teacher has 189 stamps and gives 7 to each child. How many children are there in the class?

8. The farmer's wife packs 420 eggs, and puts 12 in each box. How many boxes must she have?

1.	70 ÷ 2 =	1.	125 ÷ 5 =
2.	60 ÷ 3 =	2.	216 ÷ 6 =
3.	80 ÷ 4 =	3.	155 ÷ 5 =
4.	72 ÷ 2 =	4.	172 ÷ 4 =
5.	57 ÷ 3 =	5.	234 ÷ 6 =
6.	96 ÷ 4 =	6.	192 ÷ 8 =
1.	90 ÷ 3 =	1.	124 ÷ 4 =
2.	100 ÷ 4 =	2.	102 ÷ 3 =
3.	84 ÷ 2 =	3.	160 ÷ 5 =
4.	76 ÷ 4 =	4.	216 ÷ 3 =
5.	95 ÷ 5 =	5.	296 ÷ 8 =
6.	69 ÷ 3 =	6.	364 ÷ 7 =

II. DIVISION BY SHARING

1. CONCRETE SITUATIONS

1. In preparation for attacking this second aspect of division, and by way of breaking ground for concrete situations a few days ahead, the teacher may suggest that a collection be made of some of the objects in vogue, e.g. acorns, conkers, cigarette cards. On a certain date, the collection is to be closed, and then the announcement is made that their treasures are going to be shared up by the children, amongst the groups in the class. The leaders of each group will come to the front, so that the whole class may see that a square deal takes place, as the teacher (or a child) passes along the line sharing out the spoils. When each group's share has been assigned, another

experience will be given as these amounts are further shared out to each individual in the group.

Again, this may be made the occasion of finding out more about that interpretation of division sums with which the children are already familiar, and as they examine the amounts collected and the ways in which these have been meted out, the connection between the two methods will begin to dawn upon them.

2. Following on from this concrete example, others, using the method of drawing, may be taken together with the writing of the mathematical signs :—

(i) Share 20 oranges amongst 4 girls.

(ii) 16 shillings divided equally among two boys. How much did each boy have?

This last example will bring home to the children the idea of fractional division, and the next series may be stated as follows :—

(iii) $\frac{1}{2}$ of 20 nuts.

(iv) $\frac{1}{4}$ of 24 acorns.

(v) $\frac{1}{6}$ of 30 crackers.

MULTIPLICATION AND DIVISION

II. CONCRETE MATERIAL

With the Tillich's apparatus, again, the truth of division by sharing may be demonstrated.

ARRANGEMENT OF APPARATUS.

1. 63 ÷ 3

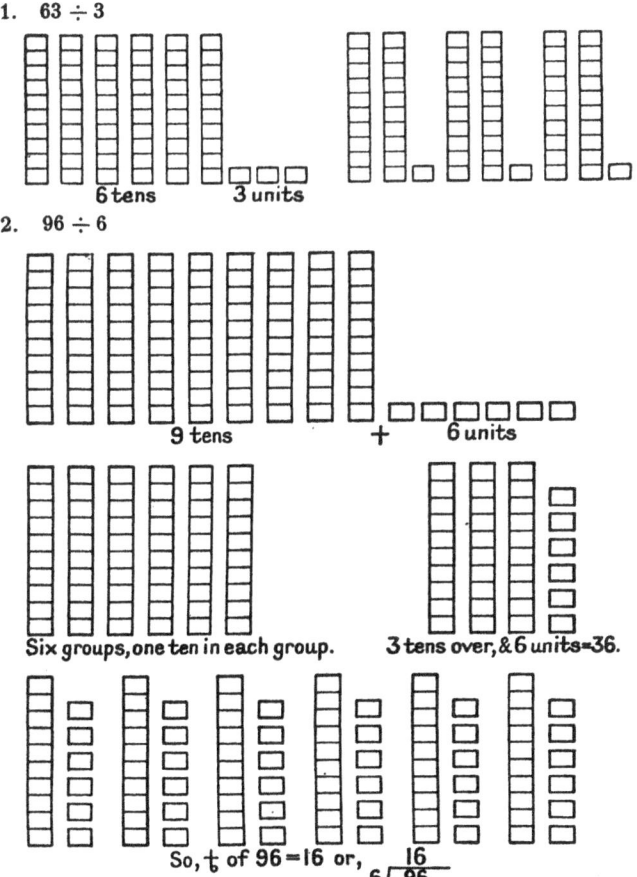

2. 96 ÷ 6

9 tens   +   6 units

Six groups, one ten in each group.   3 tens over, & 6 units = 36.

So, $\frac{1}{6}$ of 96 = 16 or, $6\overline{)96}^{\,16}$

1. $\frac{1}{3}$ of 63. See diagram 1.

First share out the tens into 3 equal parts; 6 tens ÷ 3 = 2 tens. Then share out the units into 3 equal parts; 3 ÷ 3 = 1. So, $\frac{1}{3}$ of 63 = 21, or,

$$21\\3\overline{)63}$$

III. INDIVIDUAL OCCUPATIONS

"Story" Sums.

1. Five boys buy a Meccano outfit which costs 55s. How much must each boy pay if they share alike?

2. The flower seller had 42 roses in her basket. She sold $\frac{1}{3}$ of them. How many did she sell?

3. Three boys buy a bicycle for 39s. How much must each boy pay if they share alike?

4. Rosie has 48 eggs to sell. She sells $\frac{1}{2}$ of them. How many has she sold?

5. Peter takes out 36 bundles of fire wood. He sells $\frac{1}{3}$ of them. How many has he sold?

6. Mark picks up 154 acorns, and gives away $\frac{1}{2}$. How many does he give away?

7. A sheet of penny stamps has 96 stamps. One customer buys $\frac{1}{2}$ of the sheet. How many does he buy, and how many are left?

8. Poppy has to plant 72 bulbs in her garden. She has to go to school when she has planted $\frac{1}{4}$. How many has she planted?

1. $\frac{1}{2}$ of 24 nuts.	1. $\frac{1}{2}$ of 40.
2. $\frac{1}{3}$ of 51 marbles.	2. $\frac{1}{4}$ of 36.
3. $\frac{1}{4}$ of 44 buns.	3. $\frac{1}{2}$ of 48.
4. $\frac{1}{3}$ of 27 beads.	4. $\frac{1}{5}$ of 35.
5. $\frac{1}{6}$ of 48 oranges.	5. $\frac{1}{6}$ of 66.

MULTIPLICATION AND DIVISION

1. ¼ of 32 apples.
2. ⅓ of 24 oranges.
3. ⅛ of 72 stamps.
4. ⅕ of 45 bulbs.
5. ⅐ of 49 plates.
6. ½ of 82 marbles.

1. ½ of 54.
2. ⅓ of 57.
3. ¼ of 60.
4. ⅕ of 40.
5. ⅙ of 54.
6. ⅛ of 72.

MULTIPLICATION AND DIVISION OF MONEY

The children of the Infant School will have gained the background necessary for an understanding of multiplication and division of money, in the varied experiences of their shopping and other plays. Such experiences as buying 2 lb. of tea at 1s. 8d. per lb., ½ doz. oranges at 2s. a dozen, 4 yards of material at 1s. 2d. per yard, will strengthen the children's power to comprehend the term "times" while giving them much practice in the conversion of units of measurement. But it is advisable to postpone the study of these two processes until the Junior School is reached, having the assurance that the revision of the accumulated experiences will provide a good starting-point.

Thus, the scope of the arithmetic scheme, as outlined by the experts in the section on the teaching of the subject in the Infant and Nursery School Report, will have been covered. From this Report we learn that " Most children will, before the age of 8, have acq :red at least the power to work straightforward sums the fundamental processes, and in money. . . . Refusal to recognize and make use of this experience (i.e. the experiences gained through living arithmetic) can only result in cramping the natural growth of the child."

The Report thus upholds the view expressed by recent investigators, that the study of arithmetic is not found to be " tedious or useless ", in those schools where the teaching of the subject is based on the children's interests. If concrete situations are handled in such ways, that they proceed by almost natural development to the study of processes in the concrete forms, the vital link is forged between the concrete and abstract aspects of arithmetic, and the child gains the confidence necessary for dealing with the fundamental operations of $+$, $-$, $\times$, $\div$.

CHAPTER XIV
SOME PRACTICAL SUGGESTIONS

It will be realized by many teachers that careful thought and planning will be needed to make provision for the stowing away of all the materials and apparatus for Number work. The apparatus, especially that necessary for the second and third stages in teaching processes—the concrete material and occupations for individual practice—should be kept separate from all the other school stock.

Much time will be saved by keeping this Number apparatus apart, and it will be shown that there are other considerations of accuracy and exactness involved.

I. CONCRETE MATERIAL

A shelf kept for this material will save much labour, and the materials should be kept solely for the lessons in which the aim is to study and discover principles and processes, e.g. scales and weights must be perfect if the children are to build up their table of weight, and this accuracy cannot be assured if the balances used in shopping plays are put to the test in the Number lesson.

On the arithmetic shelf, the following material should be stored :—

1. *Imitation Money.*—(i) Good cardboard coins of the exact size in imitation of the metals used, and

stamped with the king's head should be provided in preference to the paper cut-outs made by the children for their play experiences.

(ii) Treasury notes of the exact size and colour, and bearing the essential features of the Treasury notes.

2. *Measures.*—(i) Foot rules marked in three ways : (*a*) In inches ; (*b*) in inches and $\frac{1}{2}$ inches ; (*c*) in inches, $\frac{1}{2}$ and $\frac{1}{4}$ inches.

(ii) Yard Measures : (*a*) The yard, marked in fractions of the $\frac{1}{2}$, $\frac{1}{4}$, and $\frac{3}{4}$ yard ; (*b*) the yard measure, marked in feet ; (*c*) the yard measure, marked in inches ; (*d*) the yard measure combining (*a*), (*b*), (*c*).

3. *Large Clock Faces.*—(*a*) These should be about 15 inches in diameter, marked with the figures 1-12, for telling hours, $\frac{1}{2}$, and $\frac{1}{4}$ hours only ; (*b*) with the minutes added.

4. *Hour Glasses.*

5. *The Calendar for the Year.*

6. *Scales and Weights.*—The 1 lb., $\frac{1}{2}$, $\frac{1}{4}$ lb. ; 2 oz., 1 oz., $\frac{1}{2}$ oz.

7. *Milk Bottles.*—Quart, pint, $\frac{1}{2}$ pint, gill.

8. *Notation and the First Four Rules.*—Dried goods : Peas, beans, nuts ; bundles of sticks in tens, and single sticks ; Tillich's apparatus ; Abacus.

II. INDIVIDUAL OCCUPATIONS

These are best stored in the cupboard, or on shelves, away from dust and germs. Wall-pockets, and such-like

SOME PRACTICAL SUGGESTIONS 241

methods of storing are to be discouraged as unhygienic and ugly. The enterprising teacher might improvise an " apparatus wagon ", after the manner of a dinner wagon, by nailing box lids in tiers to four upright laths. The apparatus can then be covered with cloths when not in use.

CLASS ORGANIZATION

" Most teachers find that they succeed best with a composite method in which class, group, and individual training and teaching each play their part " (Infant and Nursery School Report, p. 92).

Most teachers would admit that individual teaching is the ideal, but those who are striving to base their curriculum on play methods are bound to admit that there is not time for this in the large class if there is to be *true* teaching. It may be possible to *show* or *tell* each child how to work processes, but for sound teaching, the child must be put in the position of a *discoverer*, and this takes time for both teacher and taught. As an economy of time, freeing the teacher for living and playing with the children, most teachers will agree with the above recommendation of the Ministry of Education.

In large classes, it will always be possible to break up the children into groups—the red, green, blue, etc. groups—each known by its group colour of braid or ribbon, worn as a band stretching from the left-hand shoulder transversely across the chest and back, to the right-hand side of the waist.

As the need for number lessons arises, the teacher may choose one of the three following ways for giving her definite lessons :—

(1) Dealing with each group in turn, she may give one or more lessons, sending the children to individual work when the process in question has been grasped.

(2) One lesson may be given to the class as a whole, after which the brightest children proceed to work by themselves. On a second occasion, another lesson will be given, and from the remnant, another group should be found ready and able to turn to individual work.

In this way, by a process of elimination, the teacher arrives at the dullest group, and can help them to solve their difficulties.

(3) In the writer's opinion, the most successful way of dealing with the large class is to give a first lesson to the *dullest* and *slowest* children. In the second lesson, this group is joined by the next group of quicker and slightly brighter children. The two groups go over the same work, new to group B, and now dawning on the intelligence of group C. By the time that group A (the brightest children) join the class ; group C is not only able to keep its head above water, but is able, with groups B and A, to make some intelligent contributions to the subject in hand.

Organizing in this way saves some dull children from lazy-mindedness and feelings of inferiority, and the brightest children are prevented from adopting an attitude of superiority to their weaker brothers.

WRITTEN WORK

This again is a debatable subject, for some teachers prefer to give no written work till 7 years of age, while others would let the children begin at 5 years. The surest and safest time is to begin, as the Infant and Nursery School Report advises, " when he (the child) wants to do so." Suggestions for simplifying, and making more difficult forms of written work have been given in the various chapters.

Some children, appearing to find satisfaction in their power over the pencil, prefer written work to handling material, and will find their way to principles in writing by long, tedious, and roundabout methods. Lavender, busy with her sum book at home, was heard by her father to remark, " Each of these sums takes six pages of my book." How many sixpences are there in 17s. 6d.? was the example under consideration, and the answer was found by repeated subtraction, and a final count of the sixpences. The offer to show a shorter method was rejected with the self-contained remark, " I like long sums, I like to take six pages for a sum." The working of six such examples served to show Lavender that there was something to be said for shortened methods, but nevertheless she had discovered this need for herself.

The golden rule should be to find out the children's ways of working, and to step in when their own experiences have convinced them that grown-ups have something to offer.

Problems

> "These 'problems' so far from presenting any serious difficulty to him, will constantly make his work easier, since they will keep before him the concrete aspect of the number-relations with which he has to deal."—*The Groundwork of Arithmetic*, p. 109.

How different from the sickening feeling of helpless terror of the child when confronted with the "problem" exercise which followed the mechanical work of the old text-book! To-day the child delights in problems which spring from his interests in play situations. He faces them as a means of bringing to the fore his powers of effort and love of overcoming that which offers him resistance.

Problems in play, and problems in "story" sums are alike attractive, and the latter is also a great help in giving reading practice. I have known two boys of $6\frac{1}{2}$ years learn to read through the interest aroused in "story" sums, whereas reading matter connected with their play interests had failed to arouse any desire for the tool. Ronald, a year later, had acquired the art entirely through "story" sums, and then chose for his second reading book the Bible.

The children should be encouraged to make up their own problems. "Make up a story about those numbers," said a teacher, and the child's comprehension of the meaning of her example was proved by her invention.

"$37 + 48 + 23$
37 people went to Church one Sunday
48 ,, ,, another Sunday
23 ,, ,, ,, ,,
How many people went to Church on the three Sundays?"

SOME PRACTICAL SUGGESTIONS 245

But Betty's interest and understanding of human nature was as great as her interest in number, for her next make-up produced this :—

" 435 + 181 + 235
435 people went to a Whist Drive on Monday,
181 ,, ,, ,, ,, Tuesday,
235 ,, ,, ,, ,, Wednesday.

How many people went to Whist Drives on the 3 nights ? "

The suggestion of making their own sum cards or arithmetic books may help to motivate composition when the children begin to desire to write something. Dennis undertook to compile a book of sums on Post Office life, and these two examples—a first and later attempt—show his progress.

1. A boy worked in a post office and he got 3£ a week how much did he get in 3 weeks.

2. Once there was a boy and he was very poor and he worked in a Post Office and he got 3£ a week. Anyhow he did do cross word puzzles and he won 1000£ and he married and they had a babe and it was a smiling child and a cheery child. And the child grew up and he worked in a Post Office, and he got better paid than his father. He got 5£ a week how much did he get in 4 weeks.

CONCLUSION.

Why should the school days be regarded as bringing to a full stop the child's pre-school delights? In our first chapter, we noticed the early pleasure of the little child in Number, and if this book helps the teacher to connect up that interest with the ordered ways of Number in later life, it will not have been written in vain.

To show the child, by using its own interests worked out in its own experiences, that there is rhythm in the reasoning of the mathematician, and not vexation and puzzledom so often ending in the staggering misconception of later years, is indeed a work of creative art for the teacher. It calls for strenuous effort, but repays a hundredfold.

One of the great teachers of the Victorian days said that " We have more mathematics than ever, but less mathesis." If our children can *play* and *work* as they were intended to, they will gain their mathematical foundations with much mental discipline (or mathesis) of value in every way to the child's whole being.

INDEX

A

Addition, 47 ff, 79, 84, 90 ff., 92, 96, 183 ff.; of Money, 200 ff.
Area, 25, 31, 37 f.
Arithmetic, 6, 86 ff., 105
Attention, 13, 91
Avoirdupois, 145 ff.

B

Babylonia, 169 ff.
Balance, 25, 33, 145 f.
Bills, 65 ff.

C

Calculating Boards, 172 ff., 187, 191 ff.
Caldwell Cook, *The Play Way*, 5, 13.
China, 169 ff.
Christmas, 78, 107, 219, 226 f.
Circles, 74 f., 79, 82
Class Teaching, 61, 65, 241
Class Organization, 241 ff.
Clock, 21 ff., 125 ff., 240
Collections, 233
Concrete Material, 2, 5, 10, 12, 239
  For Avoirdupois, 145 ff.
  Addition and Subtraction, 96 ff., 183 ff., 191; of Money, 200, 205
  Calendar, 134
  Capacity, 151
  Clock, 126 ff.
  Division, 230, 235
  Dozen, 106
  Foot Rule, 119 ff.
  Fractions, 159 f.
  Linear Measure, 141
  Multiplication, 220
  Multiplication Tables, 214.
  Notation, 167 f., 172.
  Shilling, 109, 113
Concrete Situations, 10, 12
  For Avoirdupois, 145
  Addition and Subtraction, 90 ff., 183 ff., 189 f.; of Money, 200, 205
  Calendar, 134
  Capacity, 150
  Clock, 125
  Division, 227 ff., 233 ff.
  Dozen, 106
  Foot Rule, 117 ff.
  Fractions, 157 f.
  Linear Measure, 140
  Multiplication, 219
  Multiplication Tables, 211
  Notation, 165, 168 ff., 181
  Shilling, 107, 111.
Constructive Interests—
  Building, 18, 26 ff., 41 ff., 83 ff.
  Drawing and Painting, 19, 23, 27, 35, 41, 70 ff., 77, 81, 113, 153, 203 f., 208 f., 212 ff., 220, 228 ff., 234
  Modelling, 27, 29, 32 ff., 41, 70 ff., 80, 106, 147, 227
  Paper and Cardboard, 23 f., 28 ff., 32 ff., 37, 46, 68 ff., 77 ff., 81 ff., 85, 106, 119 ff., 134, 140 ff., 204, 208, 212 ff., 226 f.
  Textiles, 69, 73 ff.
  Waste Material, 26 ff., 29, 32 ff., 35, 42, 68 ff., 79 ff., 82 ff.

INDEX

Counting, 1, 18 f., 21 ff., 31 ff., 36, 38, 41, 45 ff., 48 ff., 69 ff., 72, 164, 166 ff.

D

Dewey, Professor, 6, 8, 10, 61, 88, 108
Division, 77 ff., 224
  By Measuring, 225 ff.
  By Sharing, 164, 225 ff.
  Of Money, 237
Dominoes, 55
Dozen, 80, 104, 106
Dramatic Properties, 88 ff., 140, 158, 227

E

Egypt, 169 ff.
Estate Agent, 181 f., 200, 205
Experiences, 5, 10, 63

F

Figure Writing, 70, 72 f., 77
Findlay, Professor, 61
Flowers, 25, 35
Foot Rules, 104, 117 ff., 121, 240
Fractions, 70 ff., 141 ff., 148, 156 ff.
Freedom, 14

G

Games, 15, 50 ff., 183, 189
  For Ears and Eyes, 52
  For Floor—
    Allotments, 118
    Desert Island, 118
    Fish Ponds, 93
    Hop Scotch, 91
    Number Arch, 93
    Skittles, 94
    Spinning Tops, 94
  For Groups—
    Marching, 52
    Nuts and May, 51
    Oranges and Lemons, 51
    Soldier Boy, 51
  For Table or Desk—
    Cards, 55 ff., 101 f., 198, 217
    Clock, 218
    Circle games, 197
    Diddle-me-dot, 96
    Dog and Bone, 95
    Follow my Leader, 178
    Lotto, 178, 196, 217
    Racing, 96
    Spinning Discs, 95
Grouping, 34, 42, 46, 49, 51 f., 72 ff., 80 97, 107, 164
Group Lessons, 61, 65, 241

H

Habit Training, 184, 205
Hour Glass, 129, 240

I

Imitation, 28
Infant and Nursery School Report, 14, 60 f., 86, 237 f., 241, 243
Interests, 1, 5, 15, 61, 87 f. *See also* Constructive, Games, Play, Projects, Rhythmic, Story Interests.
Individual Occupations, 11 f., 53, 240
  For Avoirdupois, 149
  Addition and Subtraction, 100 ff., 195 ff.
  Calendar, 136 ff.
  Clock, 132 ff.
  Division, 232, 236
  Dozen, 107
  Foot Rule, 122 ff.
  Fractions, 161 ff.
  Linear Measure, 144 ff.

INDEX

Multiplication and Division, 223
Multiplication Tables, 216
Notation, 177 ff.
Nursery Schools, 53 ff.
Scoring Games, 101 ff.
Shilling, 113 ff.

Multiplication—
Of Money, 237
Tables, 42, 70, 77 ff., 82, 132, 211 ff., 219 ff.
Table Book, 215
Table Square, 216

J

Jig-Saw Puzzles, 101, 195, 217
Jingles, 1, 15
Jumping, 117

K

Knowledge, 216, 224

L

Linear Measure, 140 ff.
Lines, 19, 82, 84

M

Magic Squares, 101, 197
Maps, 78
Mathesis, 244
Mathematical Concepts, 1, 4
Measure of Capacity, 18, 23, 25 ff., 33, 36, 67, 71, 150 ff.
Measurement, 1, 23 ff., 31 ff., 36, 38, 41, 46 f., 54, 68 ff., 70 ff., 76, 78 ff., 83 ff., 117 ff.
Methods—
Formal, 2, 10, 91, 103 f., 156
Individual, 4
Informal, 10, 15
Project, 6 ff., 61
Memory, 10 ff., 224
Money, 31, 45 ff., 57, 80, 200 ff., 239 f.
Charts, 203 f., 208

N

Notation, 84, 104, 164 ff., 240
Number—
Chart, 89
Names, 168
Pictures, 101
Programmes, 58 f.
Writing, 169, 174, 176, 180

O

Oral Lessons, 61, 121, 155

P

Picture-study, 169
Plans, 71 ff.
Play Interests and Projects—
Building, 18, 26 ff., 35, 41 ff., 62, 83 ff., 117, 181 f., 200, 220
Bank, 83, 182, 200, 205
Cooking, 25, 145, 150
Dolls, 25 ff., 28 ff., 183, 220
Dramatizing, 20 ff., 38 ff., 84 f., 140, 165 ff., 225
Farms, 34, 220 ff.
Festivals, 42 ff., 46, 78, 113, 140, 225
Gardens, 37
Home-making, 16 ff., 23, 26 ff., 41
Post Office, 82

INDEX

Shops, 29, 31 ff., 62 ff., 106, 113, 140, 145, 150, 157, 189, 200, 219, 225 ff., 237
Street, 80 ff.
Transport, 45, 77, 107, 183 ff., 189, 200, 211, 226
Zoo, 7, 79, 117, 183, 225
Proportion, 68, 76
Punnett, *Groundwork of Arithmetic*, 244

R

Reasoning, 10, 91
Repeated Addition, 221 f.
Richman, Story of, 165
Rhymes—
  This Little Pig, 48
  There were two birds, 48
  Here is the beehive, 48
  One, two, 49
  Ten Little Nigger Boys, 50
  The Christmas Pudding, 49
  I Love Sixpence, 50
Rhythmic Interests, 15, 47 ff.
Romans, The, 171 ff.

S

Sales 67
Scale, 73 ff.
Scoring Games, 90 ff.
Shape, 23, 33 ff., 35, 42, 54, 73, 82, 84
Shilling, 104, 107 ff.
Shops, 31 ff., 57, 62 ff., 106 ff., 140, 145, 189, 200, 205, 211, 219, 237
  Confectioner, 33, 106
  Dairy, 67, 71, 106, 145, 150, 153, 157, 227
  Draper, 33, 67, 73 f., 106, 140, 158, 225, 227
  Flower, 226
  Furniture, 67, 76, 200
  Greengrocer, 33, 67, 70 f., 106, 145, 157, 226
  Grocer, 32, 67, 70 f., 106, 145, 157, 237
  House Decorator, 67, 75
  Jeweller, 69 f., 200
  Milliner, 70
  Post Office, 82 ff., 145, 211, 245
  Restaurant, 150
  Stationer, 67, 72 f., 106, 157, 226
  Sweet, 32, 67, 70, 225 f.
  Toy, 42 ff., 68 f., 140
Size, 17, 23, 31, 35, 41, 54, 71
Smith, Dr., *The Teaching of Arithmetic*, 87
Story Interests, 20 ff., 38 ff., 165
" Story " sums, 124 f., 127, 133, 136, 144, 149, 154 ff., 189 ff., 198 ff., 209 f., 223, 228 ff., 232 ff., 236, 244 f.
Storage, 240 ff.
Subtraction, 47 f., 84, 92, 98 ff., 164, 189 ff., 211 ; of Money, 205 ff.
Symbols, 55, 57, 97, 101 ff., 160 ff.
Systematic Schemes, 61, 64, 88 f.

T

Tens, 167 ff.
Tillich, 177, 179, 231, 235, 240
Time, 21 ff., 31, 70, 78, 80, 104, 128 ff., 158, 211, 219, 240
" Times," 164, 211, 219, 237
Twelve, The Measuring Unit, 103 ff.

U

Unmathematical, The, 1 f.

INDEX

V

Volume, 19

W

Weight, 1 ff., 23 ff., 33, 51, 71, 83, 146 ff., 240
Written work, 243

Y

Yard measure, 85, 211, 240
Year, 134

Z

Zero, 175 ff.
Zoo, 7, 79, 183, 227

For Product Safety Concerns and Information please contact our EU representative GPSR@taylorandfrancis.com
Taylor & Francis Verlag GmbH, Kaufingerstraße 24, 80331 München, Germany

www.ingramcontent.com/pod-product-compliance
Lightning Source LLC
Chambersburg PA
CBHW061438300426
44114CB00014B/1741